TIMED READINGS
in Literature
BOOK TWO

Edward Spargo, Editor

Selections & Questions
for this Edition:
Henry Billings
Melissa Billings

Fifty 400-Word Passages
with Questions for
Building Reading Speed

JAMESTOWN  PUBLISHERS
a division of NTC/CONTEMPORARY PUBLISHING GROUP
Lincolnwood, Illinois USA

Titles in This Series
Timed Readings, Third Edition
Timed Readings in Literature

Teaching Notes are available for this text and
will be sent to the instructor. Please write on
school stationery; tell us what grade
you teach and identify the text.

Timed Readings in Literature
Book Two

Cover and text design: Deborah Hulsey Christie

ISBN: 0-89061-515-2

Published by Jamestown Publishers,
a division of NTC/Contemporary Publishing Group, Inc.,
4255 West Touhy Avenue,
Lincolnwood (Chicago), Illinois 60712-1975 U.S.A.
11 12 13 14 15 16 17 18 19   021   08 07 06

Contents

Introduction to the Student   4

Reading Literature Faster   8

How to Use This Book   12

Instructions for the Pacing Drills   14

Timed Reading Selections   15

Answer Key   116

Progress Graph   118

Pacing Graph   120

Introduction to the Student

These *Timed Readings in Literature* are designed to help you become a faster and better reader. As you progress through the book, you will find yourself growing in reading speed and comprehension. You will be challenged to increase your reading rate while maintaining a high level of comprehension.

Reading, like most things, improves with practice. If you practice improving your reading speed, you will improve. As you will see, the rewards of improved reading speed will be well worth your time and effort.

Why Read Faster?

The quick and simple answer is that faster readers are better readers. Does this statement surprise you? You might think that fast readers would miss something and their comprehension might suffer. This is not true, for two reasons:

1. Faster readers comprehend faster. When you read faster, the writer's message is coming to you faster and makes sense sooner. Ideas are interconnected. The writer's thoughts are all tied together, each one leading to the next. The more quickly you can see how ideas are related to each other, the more quickly you can comprehend the meaning of what you are reading.

2. Faster readers concentrate better. Concentration is essential for comprehension. If your mind is wandering you can't understand what you are reading. A lack of concentration causes you to re-read, sometimes over and over, in order to comprehend. Faster readers concentrate better because there's less time for distractions to interfere. Comprehension, in turn, contributes to concentration. If you are concentrating and comprehending, you will not become distracted.

Want to Read More?

Do you wish that you could read more? (or, at least, would you like to do your required reading in less time?) Faster reading will help.

The illustration on the next page shows the number of books someone might read over a period of ten years. Let's see what faster reading could

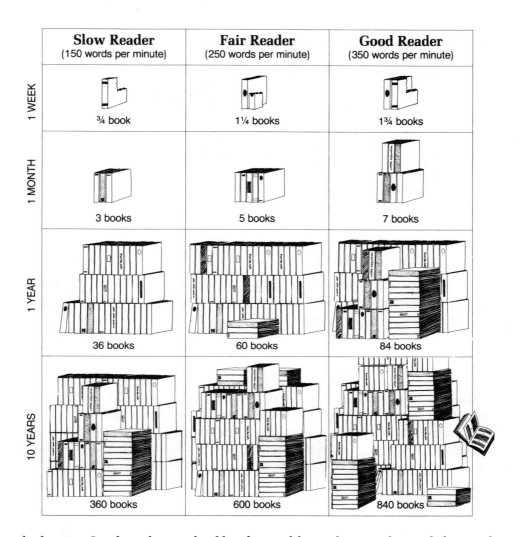

Slow Reader (150 words per minute)	Fair Reader (250 words per minute)	Good Reader (350 words per minute)
1 WEEK		
¾ book	1¼ books	1¾ books
1 MONTH		
3 books	5 books	7 books
1 YEAR		
36 books	60 books	84 books
10 YEARS		
360 books	600 books	840 books

do for you. Look at the stack of books read by a slow reader and the stack read by a good reader. (We show a speed of 350 words a minute for our "good" reader, but many fast readers can more than double that speed.) Let's say, however, that you are now reading at a rate of 150 words a minute. The illustration shows you reading 36 books a year. By increasing your reading speed to 250 words a minute, you could increase the number of books to 60 a year.

We have arrived at these numbers by assuming that the readers in our illustration read for one hour a day, six days a week, and that an average book is about 72,000 words long. Many people do not read that much, but they might if they could learn to read better and faster.

Faster reading doesn't *take* time, it *saves* time!

Acquisitional *vs.* Recreational Reading

Timed Readings in Literature gives practice in a certain kind of reading: recreational reading. Recreational reading of novels and short stories is different from the kind of reading you must employ with textbooks. You read a textbook to *acquire* facts and information. That is acquisitional reading, reading that is careful and deliberate—you cannot afford to miss something you may be quizzed on later. Acquisitional reading speed must be slower than recreational reading speed.

The practice you will be doing in this book will help you develop a high reading speed suitable for literature.

Why Practice on Literature?

If acquisitional reading is so useful and important for students, why should you spend valuable class time learning to read literature faster? Shouldn't you be learning to read textbooks faster and better? Believe it or not, you are! That's right: the reading speed and skills you develop from this book will transfer to your textbooks and to other study reading. Here are some of the ways this happens.

1. The practice effect. In the dictionary, *practice* is defined as systematic exercise to gain proficiency. In other words, repeated drill brings improvement. You know from your own experience that when you practice anything—from piano to basketball—you become better at it. The same holds true for reading. As you are doing the drills and exercises in these books, you are practicing *all* of your reading skills at the same time. With practice you become a fluent reader and comprehender—a better reader of everything you read.

2. Using context. Good readers are aware of context and use it to aid understanding. Context refers to the words surrounding those you are reading. Meaning, you see, does not come from a single word, or even a single sentence—it is conveyed within the whole context of what you are reading.

The language of literature is rich with meaning. The storyteller is trying to *please* the reader, not *teach* the reader. The writer wants to share feelings and experiences with the reader, to reach him or her in a personal way. As you practice reading literature, you are developing your skill in using context to extract the full measure of meaning and appreciation. These same context skills can be put to work when you are reading textbooks to help you organize facts into a meaningful body of knowledge.

3. Vocabulary growth. Our early vocabulary comes from listening—to our families, friends, television, teachers, and classmates. We learn and understand new words as we hear them being used by others. In fact, the more times we encounter a word, the better we understand it. Finally, it becomes ours, part of our permanent vocabulary of words we know and use.

As time goes by, an increasing number of words is introduced to us through recreational reading. Most of the words we know come from reading—words we have never looked up in a dictionary, but whose meanings have become clear to us through seeing them again and again until they are finally ours. Literature, the kind you will be reading in this book, provides countless opportunities for meeting and learning new words. Literature, as you have seen, also provides the context for seeing these new words used with precision and effect. As you work through the pages in this book, you will be developing a larger and stronger vocabulary—a storehouse of words that become your tools for learning.

4. Skills transfer. You are using this book to develop your ability to read literature with increased speed and comprehension. With regular practice and a little effort, you will be successful in reaching that goal.

As we mentioned, you will also be improving your context skills and building a bigger vocabulary. These are all wonderful results from using this book.

But, perhaps the greatest benefit of all is the application of these improvements to all of your reading tasks, not just literature. Using this book will make you a better reader, and *better readers read everything better.*

Reading Literature Faster

Through literature we share an experience with a writer. That experience may be presented as a conversation, a character or scene, an emotion, or an event.

Let's examine these four kinds of presentation. Let's see if there are characteristics or clues we can use to help us identify each kind. Once we know what we are expected to experience, we can read more intelligently and more quickly.

When you are working in this book, your instructor will schedule a few moments for you to preview each selection before timing begins. Use the preview time to scan the selection rapidly, looking for one of the following kinds of presentation.

1. Reading and Understanding a Conversation

A conversation is intended to tell us what characters are thinking or feeling—the best way to do this is through their own words.

Read the following conversation between George and his mother, an excerpt from "George's Mother" by Stephen Crane:

> Finally he said savagely: "Damn these early hours!" His mother jumped as if he had thrown a missile at her. "Why, George—" she began.
>
> George broke in again. "Oh, I know all that—but this gettin' up in th' mornin' so early just makes me sick. Jest when a man is gettin' his mornin' nap he's gotta get up. I—"
>
> "George, dear," said his mother, "yeh know I hate yeh to swear, dear. Now, please don't." She looked beseechingly at him.
>
> He made a swift gesture. "Well, I ain't swearin', am I?" he demanded. "I was only sayin' that this gettin'-up business gives me a pain, wasn't I?"
>
> "Well, yeh know how swearin' hurts me," protested the little old woman. She seemed about to sob. She gazed off . . . apparently recalling persons who had never been profane.

First, is this a conversation? Yes, we know it is. There are quotation marks throughout indicating words spoken by the characters. So, to identify a conversation, we look for quotation marks.

Next, does this conversation tell us what the characters are thinking or feeling? It certainly does—this conversation is unmistakably clear. We know how George *feels* about getting up in the morning, and we know how his mother *feels* about profanity.

8

Finally, how should we read this and other conversations we encounter in literature? Join the conversation; pretend you are one of the speakers and that these are your own words. Listen to the other character as though words are being addressed to you.

Conversations can be read quickly and understood well when you recognize them and become part of them.

2. Reading About and Understanding a Character or Scene

How do we learn about a character? There are many ways. Writers introduce characters (1) by telling us what they look like; (2) by what they say; (3) by the things they do; and (4) by telling us what others think and say about them:

> He was a staid, placid gentleman, something past the prime of life, yet upright in his carriage for all that, and slim as a greyhound. He was well mounted upon a sturdy chestnut cob, and had the graceful seat of an experienced horseman; while his riding gear, though free from such fopperies as were then in vogue, was handsome and well chosen. He wore a riding coat of a somewhat brighter green than might have been expected to suit the taste of a gentleman of his years, with a short, black velvet cape, and laced pocket holes and cuffs, all of a jaunty fashion; his linen too, was of the finest kind, worked in a rich pattern at the wrists and throat, and scrupulously white. Although he seemed, judging from the mud he had picked up on the way, to have come from London, his horse was as smooth and cool as his own iron-gray periwig and pigtail.

Obviously a character is being introduced to us in this passage from *Barnaby Rudge* by Charles Dickens. We are told how he carries himself and how he is dressed. We even know a little about what he has been doing.

The question to ask yourself is: Is this character lifelike and real? Real characters should be like real people—good and bad, happy and sad, alike and different. In reading about characters, look for the same details you look for in all people.

Similarly, when a scene or location is being described, look for words which tell about size, shape, color, appearance. Such descriptor words help us picture in our minds the place being described. Try to visualize the scene as you read.

3. Experiencing an Emotion Through Literature

When a writer presents an emotion for us to experience, the intent is to produce an effect within us. The intended effect may be pity, fear, revulsion, or some other emotion. The writer wants us to *feel* something.

In the following passage from *Jane Eyre* by Charlotte Brontë, what emotions are we expected to feel for the character?

> John had not much affection for his mother and sisters, and an antipathy to me. He bullied and punished me; not two or three times in the week, not once or twice in the day, but continually: every nerve I had feared him, and every morsel of flesh on my bones shrank when he came near. There were moments when I was bewildered by the terror he inspired, because I had no appeal whatever against either his menaces or his inflictions; the servants did not like to offend their young master by taking my part against him, and Mrs. Reed was blind and deaf on the subject: She never saw him strike or heard him abuse me, though he did both now and then in her very presence; more frequently behind her back.

Do you feel sorry for this girl because she is being abused? Do you feel compassion because she is suffering? Are you suffering with her? Do you feel anger toward her abuser? What other effects are intended? How are these effects produced?

Emotional and provocative words and expressions have been employed by the writer to paint a vivid portrait of her character's predicament. Can you identify some of the words? What did John do? He *bullied, struck, punished,* and *abused.* The girl felt fear, bewilderment, and terror. These very expressive and emotional words and phrases are the clues provided by the writer to help her readers read and comprehend effectively.

4. Reading About and Understanding an Event

In describing an event—a series of actions—the writer is telling us a story, and the elements of the story are presented in some kind of order or pattern. Read this passage from *Around the World in Eighty Days* by Jules Verne:

> Mr. Fogg and his two companions took their places on a bench opposite the desks of the magistrate and his clerk. Immediately after, Judge Obadiah, a fat, round man, followed by the clerk, entered. He proceeded to take down a wig which was hanging on a nail, and put it hurriedly on his head.
>
> "The first case," said he. Then, putting his hand to his head, he exclaimed "Heh! This is not my wig!"
>
> "No, your worship," returned the clerk, "it is mine."
>
> "My dear Mr. Oysterpuff, how can a judge give a wise sentence in a clerk's wig?"
>
> The wigs were exchanged.

Did you see how this little story was told? The events in the story were presented in chronological order—from first to last as they occurred. This is a frequently used and easily recognized pattern, but not the only one writers use. The story could have been told in reverse—the story could have opened with the judge wearing the wrong wig and then gone on to explain how the mistake happened.

In passages like these, look for the events in the story and see how they are related, how one event follows or builds on the other. By recognizing the pattern of storytelling and using the pattern as an aid to organizing and understanding the events, you can become a better and faster reader.

How to Use This Book

1 Read the lessons
First, read the lessons on pages 8 through 11. These lessons teach you how to recognize and identify the kinds of presentation you encounter in literature and in the selections in this book.

2 Preview
Find a literature selection to read and wait for your instructor's signal to preview. You will have 30 seconds to preview (scan) the selection to identify the author's kind of presentation.

3 Begin reading
When your instructor gives you the signal, begin reading. Read at a slightly faster-than-normal speed. Read well enough so that you will be able to answer questions about what you have read.

7 Fill in the progress graph
Enter your score and plot your reading time on the graph on page 118 or 119. The right-hand side of the graph shows your words-per-minute reading speed. Write this number at the bottom of the page on the line labeled *Words per Minute.*

4 **Record your time**
When you finish reading, look at the blackboard and note your reading time. Your reading time will be the lowest time remaining on the board, or the next number to be erased. Write this time at the bottom of the page on the line labeled *Reading Time*.

5 **Answer the questions**
Answer the ten questions on the next page. There are five fact questions and five thought questions. Pick the *best* answer to each question and put an x in the box beside it.

6 **Correct your answers**
Using the Answer Key on pages 116 and 117, correct your work. Circle your wrong answers and put an x in the box you should have marked. Score 10 points for each correct answer. Write your score at the bottom of the page on the line labeled *Comprehension Score*.

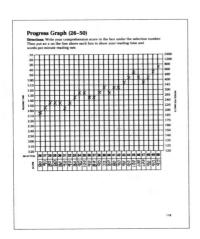

Instructions for the Pacing Drills

Pacing Dots

From time to time your instructor may wish to conduct pacing drills using *Timed Readings*. For this work you need to use the Pacing Dots printed in the margins of your book pages. The dots will help you regulate your reading speed to match the pace set by your instructor or announced on the reading cassette tape.

You will be reading at the correct pace if you are at the dot when your instructor says "Mark" or when you hear a tone on the tape. If you are ahead of the pace, read a little more slowly; if you are behind the pace, increase your reading speed. Try to match the pace exactly.

Follow these steps.

Step 1: Record the pace. At the bottom of the page, write on the line labeled *Words per Minute* the rate announced by the instructor or by the speaker on the tape.

Step 2: Begin reading. Wait for the signal to begin reading. Read at a slightly faster-than-normal speed. You will not know how on-target your pace is until you hear your instructor say "Mark" or until you hear the first tone on the tape. After a little practice you will be able to select an appropriate starting speed most of the time.

Step 3: Adjust your pace. As you read, try to match the pace set by the instructor or the tape. Read more slowly or more quickly as necessary. You should be reading the line beside the dot when you hear the pacing signal. The pacing sounds may distract you at first. Don't worry about it. Keep reading and your concentration will return.

Step 4: Stop and answer questions. Stop reading when you are told to, even if you have not finished the selection. Answer the questions right away. Correct your work and record your score on the line *Comprehension Score*. Strive to maintain 80 percent comprehension on each drill as you gradually increase your pace.

Step 5: Fill in the pacing graph. Transfer your words-per-minute rate to the box labeled *Pace* on the pacing graph on page 120. Then plot your comprehension score on the line above the box.

These pacing drills are designed to help you become a more flexible reader. They encourage you to "break out" of a pattern of reading everything at the same speed.

The drills help in other ways, too. Sometimes in a reading program you reach a certain level and bog down. You don't seem able to move on and progress. The pacing drills will help you to work your way out of such slumps and get your reading program moving again.

Tom's mind was made up now. He was gloomy and desperate. He was a forsaken, friendless boy, he said. Nobody loved him. When they found out what they had driven him to, perhaps they would be sorry. He had tried to do right and get along, but they would not let him. Since nothing would do them but to be rid of him, let it be so. Let them blame *him* for the consequences—why shouldn't they? What right had the friendless to complain? Yes, they had forced him to it at last. He would lead a life of crime. ●
There was no choice.

By this time he was far down Meadow Lane, and the bell for school to "take up" tinkled faintly upon his ear. He sobbed, now, to think he should never, never hear that old familiar sound anymore. It was very hard, but it was forced on him. Since he was driven out into the cold world, he must submit—but he forgave them. Then the sobs came thick and fast.

Just at this point he met his soul's sworn comrade, Joe Harper—hard eyed, and with evidently a great and dismal purpose in his heart. Plainly ●
here were "two souls with but a single thought." Tom began to blubber out something about a resolution to escape home by roaming abroad into the great world never to return; and ended by hoping that Joe would not forget him.

But it transpired that this was a request which Joe had just been going to make of Tom, and had come to hunt him up for that purpose. His mother had whipped him for drinking some cream which he had never tasted and knew nothing about. It was plain that she was tired of him and wished him to go. If she felt that way, there was nothing for him to do but succumb. ●
He hoped she would be happy and never regret having driven her poor boy out into the unfeeling world to suffer and die.

As the two boys walked sorrowing along, they made a new compact to stand by each other and be brothers and never separate till death relieved them of their troubles. Then they began to lay their plans. Joe was for being a hermit, and living on crusts in a remote cave, and dying, some time, of cold and want and grief.

Recalling Facts

1. Tom felt that
   □ a. things were going his way.
   □ b. nobody loved him.
   □ c. his friends were cruel.

2. Tom decided he would lead a life of
   □ a. sorrow.
   □ b. pleasure.
   □ c. crime.

3. Tom sobbed when he realized that he would never again hear the
   □ a. school bell.
   □ b. church bell.
   □ c. steamship bell.

4. Joe's mother whipped him for drinking some
   □ a. whiskey.
   □ b. cream.
   □ c. cider.

5. Joe wanted to be a
   □ a. bandit.
   □ b. hermit.
   □ c. beggar.

Understanding the Passage

6. Tom was feeling
   □ a. sorry for himself.
   □ b. anxious and excited.
   □ c. very relaxed.

7. Joe thought his mother was
   □ a. the sweetest woman in the world.
   □ b. trying to get rid of him.
   □ c. worried about money.

8. Tom and Joe
   □ a. were brothers.
   □ b. looked at the world the same way.
   □ c. were sworn and everlasting enemies.

9. Tom and Joe were planning to
   □ a. go on a long hike.
   □ b. skip school for the day.
   □ c. run away from home.

10. Joe felt that if he and Tom were "out in the world alone," they would
    □ a. have a grand time.
    □ b. suffer and die.
    □ c. get a better education.

Into this fine box the groom put me; it was clean, sweet, and airy. I never was in a better box than that, and the sides were not so high but that I could see all that went on through the iron rails that were at the top.

He gave me some very nice oats, he patted me, spoke kindly, and then went away.

When I had eaten my corn I looked round. In the stall next to mine stood a little fat gray pony, with a thick mane and tail, a very pretty head, and a pert little nose.

I put my head up to the iron rails at the top of my box, and said, "How do you do? What is your name?"

He turned round as far as his halter would allow, held up his head, and said, "My name is Merrylegs. I am very handsome; I carry the young ladies on my back, and sometimes I take our mistress out in the low chair. They think a great deal of me, and so does James. Are you going to live next door to me in the box?"

I said, "Yes."

"Well, then," he said, "I hope you are good tempered; I do not like anyone next door who bites."

Just then a horse's head looked over from the stall beyond; the ears were laid back, and the eye looked rather ill-tempered. This was a tall chestnut mare, with a long handsome neck. She looked across to me and said:

"So it is you who have turned me out of my box; it is a very strange thing for a colt like you to come and turn a lady out of her own home."

"I beg your pardon," I said, "I have turned no one out; the man who brought me put me here, and I had nothing to do with it; and as to my being a colt, I am turned four years old and am a grown-up horse. I never had words yet with horse or mare, and it is my wish to live at peace."

"Well," she said, "we shall see. Of course, I do not want to have words with a young thing like you." I said no more.

In the afternoon, when she went out, Merrylegs told me all about it.

"The thing is this," said Merrylegs. "Ginger has a bad habit of biting."

Recalling Facts

1. The animal in the next stall was a
   - ☐ a. mule.
   - ☐ b. donkey.
   - ☐ c. pony.

2. Merrylegs thought of himself as
   - ☐ a. handsome.
   - ☐ b. unwanted.
   - ☐ c. neglected.

3. The new horse was given a stall that once belonged to a
   - ☐ a. brown stallion.
   - ☐ b. grey colt.
   - ☐ c. chestnut mare.

4. The new horse was
   - ☐ a. three years old.
   - ☐ b. four years old.
   - ☐ c. five years old.

5. Ginger had a bad habit of
   - ☐ a. coughing.
   - ☐ b. kicking.
   - ☐ c. biting.

Understanding the Passage

6. The new horse seemed
   - ☐ a. sad.
   - ☐ b. happy.
   - ☐ c. angry.

7. Ginger was angry because the new horse
   - ☐ a. ate her corn.
   - ☐ b. was given her old stall.
   - ☐ c. spoke to Merrylegs.

8. The new horse did not like
   - ☐ a. arguments.
   - ☐ b. the size of his stall.
   - ☐ c. Merrylegs.

9. Ginger was
   - ☐ a. younger than the new horse.
   - ☐ b. older than the new horse.
   - ☐ c. the same age as the new horse.

10. Merrylegs did not like living next to
    - ☐ a. Ginger.
    - ☐ b. the new horse.
    - ☐ c. the groom.

Mr. Utterson was sitting by his fireside one evening after dinner, when he was surprised to receive a visit from Poole.

"Bless me, Poole, what brings you here?" he cried; and then taking a second look at him, "What ails you?" he added. "Is the doctor ill?"

"Mr. Utterson," said the man, "there is something wrong."

"Take a seat, and here is a glass of wine for you," said the lawyer. "Now, take your time, and tell me plainly what you want."

"You know the doctor's ways, sir," replied Poole, "and how he shuts himself up. Well, he's shut up again in the cabinet. I don't like it, sir—I wish I may die if I like it. Mr. Utterson, sir, I'm afraid."

"Now, my good man," said the lawyer, "be explicit. What are you afraid of?"

"I've been afraid for about a week," returned Poole, doggedly disregarding the question, "and I can bear it no more."

The man's appearance amply bore out his words. His manner was altered for the worse; and except for the moment when he had first announced his terror, he had not once looked the lawyer in the face. Even now, he sat with the glass of wine untasted on his knee, and his eyes directed to a corner of the floor. "I can bear it no more," he repeated.

"Come," said the lawyer, "I see you have some good reason, Poole. I see there is something seriously amiss. Try to tell me what it is."

"I think there's been foul play," said Poole, hoarsely.

"Foul play!" cried the lawyer, a good deal frightened. "What foul play! What does the man mean?"

"I daren't say, sir," was the answer; "but will you come along with me and see for yourself?"

Mr. Utterson's only answer was to rise and get his hat and greatcoat; but he observed with wonder the greatness of the relief that appeared upon the butler's face, and perhaps with no less, that the wine was still untasted when he set it down to follow.

It was a wild, cold night of March, with a pale moon, lying on her back as though the wind had tilted her. The wind made talking difficult, and flecked the blood into the face. It seemed to have swept the streets unusually bare of passengers.

Recalling Facts

1. Utterson offered Poole a glass of
   - ☐ a. brandy.
   - ☐ b. wine.
   - ☐ c. water.

2. The doctor had locked himself in the
   - ☐ a. attic.
   - ☐ b. basement.
   - ☐ c. cabinet.

3. Poole told Utterson that he had been afraid for about a
   - ☐ a. day.
   - ☐ b. week.
   - ☐ c. year.

4. Poole thought there had been
   - ☐ a. foul play.
   - ☐ b. a suicide.
   - ☐ c. a party.

5. This scene took place on a
   - ☐ a. hot summer evening.
   - ☐ b. windy autumn afternoon.
   - ☐ c. cold March night.

Understanding the Passage

6. Poole apparently worked for the
   - ☐ a. doctor.
   - ☐ b. butler.
   - ☐ c. lawyer.

7. Mr. Utterson was familiar with
   - ☐ a. the doctor's strange habits.
   - ☐ b. everyone in town.
   - ☐ c. the butler's fears.

8. Utterson was surprised that Poole
   - ☐ a. didn't touch his drink.
   - ☐ b. knew where to find him.
   - ☐ c. had left his employer's side.

9. Poole was happy that
   - ☐ a. the doctor was locked up.
   - ☐ b. Mr. Utterson agreed to come with him.
   - ☐ c. there were no people on the streets.

10. Poole's frame of mind can best be described as
   - ☐ a. desperate.
   - ☐ b. amused.
   - ☐ c. distracted.

"What were you thinking about just now, when you sat staring at the fire?" asked Tom.

"I was thinking about Jimmy," Polly said.

"Would you mind telling about him? You know, you said you would some time; but don't, if you'd rather not," said Tom, lowering his rough voice respectfully.

"I like to talk about him; but there isn't much to tell," began Polly, grateful for his interest. "Sitting here with you reminded me of the way I used to sit with him when he was sick. We used to have such happy times, and it's so pleasant to think about them now."

"He was awfully good, wasn't he?"

"No, he wasn't. But he tried to be, and mother says that is half the battle. We used to get tired of trying; but we kept making resolutions, and working hard to keep 'em. I don't think I got on much; but Jimmy did, and everyone loved him."

"Didn't you ever squabble, as we do?"

"Yes, indeed, sometimes; but we couldn't stay mad, and always made it up again as soon as we could. Jimmy used to come round first, and say, 'All serene, Polly,' so kind and jolly, that I couldn't help laughing and being friends right away."

"Did he not know a lot?"

"Yes, I think he did, for he liked to study, and wanted to get on, so he could help father. People used to call him a fine boy, and I felt so proud to hear it; but they didn't know half how wise he was, because he didn't show off a bit. I suppose sisters always think their brothers are grand. But I don't believe many girls had as much right to be as I had."

"Most girls don't care two pins about their brothers; so that shows you don't know much about it."

"Well, they ought to, if they don't; and they would if the boys were as kind to them as Jimmy was to me."

"Why, what did he do?"

"Loved me dearly, and wasn't ashamed to show it," cried Polly, with a sob in her voice.

"What made him die, Polly?" asked Tom, soberly, after a little pause.

"He got hurt coasting, last winter; but he never told which boy did it, and he only lived a week. I helped take care of him; and he was so patient."

Recalling Facts

1. Polly said that she was thinking about
   - ☐ a. Tom.
   - ☐ b. Jimmy.
   - ☐ c. her mother.

2. Polly said that everyone loved
   - ☐ a. her.
   - ☐ b. Tom.
   - ☐ c. Jimmy.

3. Jimmy liked to
   - ☐ a. study.
   - ☐ b. cause trouble.
   - ☐ c. show off.

4. Jimmy was Polly's
   - ☐ a. neighbor.
   - ☐ b. cousin.
   - ☐ c. brother.

5. Jimmy was hurt while
   - ☐ a. coasting.
   - ☐ b. bicycling.
   - ☐ c. hunting.

Understanding the Passage

6. Tom was curious about
   - ☐ a. Jimmy's life.
   - ☐ b. Polly's friends.
   - ☐ c. unusual diseases.

7. Jimmy sometimes
   - ☐ a. broke the law.
   - ☐ b. fought with Polly.
   - ☐ c. both a and b.

8. Jimmy and Polly both appeared to be
   - ☐ a. sneaky.
   - ☐ b. sincere.
   - ☐ c. greedy.

9. Polly felt that people didn't know just how
   - ☐ a. funny Jimmy could be.
   - ☐ b. smart Jimmy was.
   - ☐ c. dishonest Jimmy was.

10. Polly felt that her relationship with Jimmy was
    - ☐ a. unloving.
    - ☐ b. special.
    - ☐ c. boring.

Rat and Mole waited for what seemed a very long time, stamping in the snow to keep their feet warm. At last they heard the sound of slow shuffling footsteps approaching the door from the inside. It seemed, as the Mole remarked to the Rat, like someone walking in carpet slippers that were too large for him and down-at-heel. This was intelligent of Mole, because that was exactly what it was.

There was the noise of a bolt shot back, and the door opened a few inches, enough to show a long snout and a pair of sleepy blinking eyes.

"Now, the *very* next time this happens," said a gruff voice, "I shall be most angry. Who is it *this* time, disturbing people on such a night? Speak up!"

"O, Badger," cried the Rat, "let us in, please. It's me, Rat, and my friend Mole. We've lost our way in the snow."

"What, Ratty, my dear little man!" exclaimed the Badger, in quite a different voice. "Come along in, both of you, at once. Why, you must be perished. Well I never! Lost in the snow! And in the Wild Wood, too, and at this time of night! But come in with you."

The two animals tumbled over each other in their eagerness to get inside, and heard the door shut behind them with great joy and relief.

The Badger, who wore a long dressing gown, and whose slippers were indeed very down-at-heel, carried a flat candlestick in his paw. He had probably been on his way to bed when their summons sounded. He looked kindly down on them and patted both their heads. "This is not the sort of night for small animals to be out," he said paternally. "I'm afraid you've been up to some of your pranks again, Ratty. But come along; come into the kitchen. There's a first-rate fire there, and supper and everything."

He shuffled on in front of them, carrying the light, and they followed him down a long, gloomy, and, to tell the truth, shabby passage, into a sort of a central hall, out of which they could dimly see other long tunnel-like passages branching. But there were doors in the hall as well—stout oaken doors. One of these the Badger flung open, and at once they found themselves in all the glow and warmth of a large fire-lit kitchen.

Recalling Facts

1. Rat and Mole got lost in the
   - ☐ a. Great Kingdom.
   - ☐ b. Dark Forest.
   - ☐ c. Wild Wood.

2. They found shelter at the home of
   - ☐ a. Mrs. Rat.
   - ☐ b. the Badger.
   - ☐ c. the Otter.

3. Outside it was
   - ☐ a. raining.
   - ☐ b. snowing.
   - ☐ c. dreadfully hot.

4. The Badger wore
   - ☐ a. old slippers.
   - ☐ b. old boots.
   - ☐ c. wooden shoes.

5. The Badger took the Rat and Mole into his
   - ☐ a. bedroom.
   - ☐ b. kitchen.
   - ☐ c. workshop.

Understanding the Passage

6. The Badger was
   - ☐ a. bigger than Rat and Mole.
   - ☐ b. smaller than Rat and Mole.
   - ☐ c. the father of Rat and Mole.

7. Apparently, other animals had been
   - ☐ a. knocking on Badger's door.
   - ☐ b. building houses in Badger's yard.
   - ☐ c. stealing Badger's food.

8. When Badger invited them inside, Rat and Mole were very
   - ☐ a. suspicious.
   - ☐ b. disappointed.
   - ☐ c. grateful.

9. The Badger's home could best be described as
   - ☐ a. modest.
   - ☐ b. pitiful.
   - ☐ c. fabulous.

10. The Badger did not usually
    - ☐ a. use a candlestick.
    - ☐ b. keep a fire going in his kitchen.
    - ☐ c. have visitors late at night.

from **Life of Ma Parker** *by Katherine Mansfield*

That was a dreadful place—her first job. She was never allowed out. She never went upstairs except for prayers morning and evening. It was a fair cellar. And the cook was a cruel woman. She used to snatch away her letters from home before she'd read them, and throw them in the range because they made her dreamy. And the beetles! Would you believe it? Until she came to London she'd never seen a black beetle. Here Mrs. Parker always gave a little laugh, as though—not to have seen a black beetle! Well! It was as if to say you'd never seen your own feet.

When that family moved on she went as "help" to a doctor's house. After two years there, on the run from morning till night, she married her husband. He was a baker.

"A baker, Mrs. Parker!" the literary gentleman said. "It must have been rather nice to be married to a baker!"

Mrs. Parker didn't look so sure.

"Such a clean trade," said the gentleman.

Mrs. Parker didn't look convinced.

"And didn't you like handing the new loaves to the customers?"

"Well, sir," said Mrs. Parker, "I wasn't in the shop above a great deal. We had thirteen little ones and buried seven of them. If it wasn't the hospital it was the infirmary, you might say!"

"You might, *indeed*, Mrs. Parker!" said the gentleman, shuddering.

Yes, seven had gone, and while the six were still small her husband was taken ill with consumption. It was flour on the lungs, the doctor told her at the time. Her husband sat up in bed with his shirt pulled over his head, and the doctor's finger drew a circle on his back.

"Now, if we were to cut him open *here*, Mrs. Parker," said the doctor, "you'd find his lungs chock-a-block with white powder. Breathe, my good fellow!" And Mrs. Parker never knew for certain whether she saw or whether she fancied she saw a great fan of white dust come out of her poor dear husband's lips.

But the struggle she'd had to bring up those six little children. Terrible it had been! Then, just when they were old enough to go to school, her husband's sister came to help them, and she hadn't been there more than two months when she fell down a flight of steps and hurt her spine.

Recalling Facts

1. Until she came to London,
   Mrs. Parker had never seen a
   ☐ a. cellar.
   ☐ b. black beetle.
   ☐ c. bakery.

2. Mrs. Parker married a
   ☐ a. doctor.
   ☐ b. baker.
   ☐ c. literary gentleman.

3. Seven of Mrs. Parker's
   children had
   ☐ a. married doctors.
   ☐ b. not lived long.
   ☐ c. not lived below the
       bakery.

4. Mrs. Parker did not
   ☐ a. spend much time in her
       husband's shop.
   ☐ b. believe in hospitals.
   ☐ c. love her children.

5. Mrs. Parker's husband became
   ill with
   ☐ a. diphtheria.
   ☐ b. consumption.
   ☐ c. cancer.

Understanding the Passage

6. Apparently the city of
   London contained many
   ☐ a. insects.
   ☐ b. bakeries.
   ☐ c. factories.

7. Mr. Parker's doctor
   ☐ a. saved Mrs. Parker's life.
   ☐ b. treated the woman with
       the injured spine.
   ☐ c. was unable to cure his
       consumption.

8. Mrs. Parker had
   ☐ a. seen some hard times.
   ☐ b. lived a comfortable life.
   ☐ c. never lacked money.

9. The gentleman talking to
   Mrs. Parker
   ☐ a. did not know Mrs.
       Parker's life history.
   ☐ b. wanted to marry Mrs.
       Parker.
   ☐ c. volunteered to care for
       Mr. Parker.

10. The gentleman thought that
    being a baker sounded
    ☐ a. boring.
    ☐ b. pleasant.
    ☐ c. elegant.

from **White Fang** *by Jack London*

"Where are you goin'?" Henry suddenly demanded, laying his hand on his partner's arm.

Bill shook it off. "I won't stand it," he said. "They ain't a-goin' to get any more of our dogs if I can help it."

Gun in hand, he plunged into the underbrush that lined the side of the trail. His intention was apparent enough. Taking the sled as the center of the circle that One Ear was making, Bill planned to tap that circle at a point in advance of the pursuit.

With his rifle, in the broad daylight, it might be possible for him to awe the wolves and save the dog.

"Say, Bill!" Henry called after him. "Be careful! Don't take no chances!"

Henry sat down on the sled and watched. There was nothing else for him to do. Bill had already gone from sight; but now and again, appearing and disappearing amongst the underbrush and the scattered clumps of spruce, could be seen One Ear. Henry judged his case to be hopeless. The dog was thoroughly alive to its danger, but it was running on the outer circle while the wolf-pack was running on the inner and shorter circle. It was vain to think of One Ear so outdistancing his pursuers as to be able to cut across their circle in advance of them and to regain the sled.

The different lines were rapidly approaching a point. Somewhere out there in the snow, screened from his sight by trees and thickets, Henry knew that the wolf-pack, One Ear, and Bill were coming together. All too quickly, far more quickly than he had expected, it happened. He heard a shot, then two shots in rapid succession, and he knew that Bill's ammunition was gone. Then he heard a great outcry of snarls and yelps. He recognized One Ear's yell of pain and terror, and he heard a wolf cry that bespoke a stricken animal. And that was all. The snarls ceased. The yelping died away. Silence settled down again over the lonely land.

He sat for a long while upon the sled. There was no need for him to go and see what had happened. He knew it as though it had taken place before his eyes. Once, he roused with a start and hastily got the axe out from underneath the lashings. But for some time longer he sat and brooded.

Recalling Facts

1. One Ear was
   - ☐ a. an Indian warrior.
   - ☐ b. a wolf.
   - ☐ c. a dog.

2. Henry thought One Ear had
   - ☐ a. no chance of outrunning the wolves.
   - ☐ b. a good chance of outrunning the wolves.
   - ☐ c. an excellent chance of outrunning the wolves.

3. The wolf-pack was running
   - ☐ a. in a straight line.
   - ☐ b. on the outer circle.
   - ☐ c. on the shorter circle.

4. Bill fired
   - ☐ a. one shot.
   - ☐ b. two shots.
   - ☐ c. three shots.

5. Henry
   - ☐ a. ran after Bill.
   - ☐ b. stayed with the sled.
   - ☐ c. cried when he heard the shots.

Understanding the Passage

6. The wolf-pack
   - ☐ a. was a new threat.
   - ☐ b. had already killed some dogs.
   - ☐ c. just wanted to be near the campfire.

7. Henry knew that Bill
   - ☐ a. could save One Ear.
   - ☐ b. was taking a big chance.
   - ☐ c. enjoyed shooting wolves.

8. One Ear
   - ☐ a. had no idea of the danger he faced.
   - ☐ b. was trying to outrun the wolves.
   - ☐ c. managed to slip past the wolves' circle.

9. Bill and Henry were traveling through
   - ☐ a. the frozen wilderness.
   - ☐ b. sunny fields.
   - ☐ c. New England.

10. Henry believed he knew
    - ☐ a. how to save One Ear.
    - ☐ b. where to get new dogs.
    - ☐ c. the outcome of Bill's fight with the wolves.

from **Vanity Fair** *by William Makepeace Thackeray*

Sir Pitt started when he saw poor Rawdon in his study in tumbled clothes, with bloodshot eyes, and his hair over his face. Sir Pitt thought his brother was not sober, and had been out all night on some orgy. "Good gracious, Rawdon," he said, with a blank face, "what brings you here at this time of the morning? Why ain't you at home?"

"Home," said Rawdon, with a wild laugh. "Don't be frightened, Pitt. I'm not drunk. Shut the door; I want to speak to you."

Pitt closed the door and came up to the table, where he seated himself in the other armchair—the one placed for the reception of the steward, agent, or confidential visitor who came to transact business with the Baronet—and trimmed his nails more vehemently than ever.

"Pitt, it's all over with me," the Colonel said, after a pause. "I'm done."

"I always said it would come to this," the Baronet cried peevishly, and beating a tune with his clean-trimmed nails. "I warned you a thousand times. I can't help you any more. Every shilling of my money is tied up. Even the hundred pounds that Jane took you last night were promised to my lawyer tomorrow morning, and the want of it will put me to great inconvenience. I don't mean to say that I won't assist you ultimately. But as for paying your creditors in full, I might as well hope to pay the National debt. It is madness, sheer madness, to think of such a thing. You must come to a compromise. It's a painful thing for the family; but everybody does it. There was George Kitely, Lord Ragland's son, went through the Court last week, and was what they call whitewashed, I believe. Lord Ragland would not pay a shilling for him, and—"

"It's not money I want," Rawdon broke in. "I'm not come to you about myself. Never mind what happens to me—"

"What is the matter, then?" said Pitt, somewhat relieved.

"It's the boy," said Rawdon, in a husky voice. "I want you to promise me that you will take charge of him when I'm gone. That dear good wife of yours has always been good to him, and he's fonder of her than he is of his . . . damn it. Look here, Pitt: you know that I was to have had Miss Crawley's money."

Recalling Facts

1. Sir Pitt was Rawdon's
   - ☐ a. business partner.
   - ☐ b. drinking partner.
   - ☐ c. brother.

2. Rawdon's military rank was
   - ☐ a. lieutenant.
   - ☐ b. captain.
   - ☐ c. colonel.

3. While Rawdon talked, Pitt
   - ☐ a. paced the room.
   - ☐ b. trimmed his nails.
   - ☐ c. left the room.

4. The hundred pounds given to Rawdon had been
   - ☐ a. promised to Pitt's lawyer.
   - ☐ b. set aside for Jane's education.
   - ☐ c. due him for a long time.

5. Rawdon said his real concern was
   - ☐ a. for the boy.
   - ☐ b. getting his creditors paid off.
   - ☐ c. to help his troubled wife.

Understanding the Passage

6. When Pitt first saw Rawdon, he thought he was
   - ☐ a. dying.
   - ☐ b. drunk.
   - ☐ c. celebrating.

7. Pitt apparently
   - ☐ a. often found Rawdon in trouble.
   - ☐ b. wanted to help Rawdon any way he could.
   - ☐ c. was responsible for Rawdon's problems.

8. Pitt thought that Rawdon should
   - ☐ a. pay off his creditors in full.
   - ☐ b. turn himself in to the police.
   - ☐ c. strike a deal to pay off some of his debts.

9. Pitt was relieved when Rawdon
   - ☐ a. asked for only a little money.
   - ☐ b. asked for Miss Crawley's money.
   - ☐ c. said he wouldn't ask for money.

10. The boy mentioned in the passage appears to be
    - ☐ a. Pitt's son.
    - ☐ b. Rawdon's son.
    - ☐ c. Pitt's younger brother.

Ramona proceeded to Felipe's room. Felipe was sleeping, the Señora sitting by his side, as she had sat for days and nights, her dark face looking thinner and more drawn each day; her hair looking even whiter, if that could be; and her voice growing hollow from faintness and sorrow.

"Dear Señora," whispered Ramona, "do go out for a few moments while he sleeps, and let me watch—just on the walk in front of the veranda. The sun is still lying there, bright and warm. You will be ill if you do not have air."

The Señora shook her head. "My place is here," she answered, speaking in a dry, hard tone. Sympathy was hateful to the Señora; she wished neither to give it nor take it. "I shall not leave him. I do not need the air."

Ramona had a cloth-of-gold rose in her hand. The veranda eaves were now shaded with them, hanging down like a thick fringe of golden tassels. It was the rose Felipe loved best. Stooping, she laid it on the bed, near Felipe's head. "He will like to see it when he wakes," she said.

The Señora seized it, and flung it far out in the room. "Take it away! Flowers are poison when one is ill," she said coldly. "Have I never told you that?"

"No, Señora," replied Ramona, meekly; and she glanced at the saucer of musk which the Señora kept on the table close to Felipe's pillow.

"The musk is different," said the Señora, seeing the glance. "Musk is a medicine. It revives."

Ramona knew, but she would have never dared to say, that Felipe hated musk. Many times he had said to her how he hated the odor; but his mother was so fond of it, that it must always be that the veranda and the house would be full of it. Ramona hated it too. At times it made her faint. But neither she nor Felipe would have confessed as much to the Señora. And if they had, she would have thought it all a fancy.

"Shall I stay?" asked Ramona, gently.

"As you please," replied the Señora. The presence of Ramona irked her now with a feeling she did not pretend to analyze, and would have been terrified at if she had. She would not have dared to say to herself, in plain words: "why is that girl well and strong, and my Felipe lying here to die?"

Recalling Facts

1. Felipe was
   - ☐ a. dead.
   - ☐ b. sleeping.
   - ☐ c. awake.

2. Ramona offered to
   - ☐ a. relieve the Señora.
   - ☐ b. make dinner.
   - ☐ c. change the bedding.

3. Next to Felipe's head, Ramona tried to place
   - ☐ a. golden tassels.
   - ☐ b. a bible.
   - ☐ c. a rose.

4. The Señora believed in the healing power of
   - ☐ a. musk.
   - ☐ b. flowers.
   - ☐ c. sunshine.

5. The presence of Ramona
   - ☐ a. pleased the Señora.
   - ☐ b. irked the Señora.
   - ☐ c. was ignored by the Señora.

Understanding the Passage

6. Ramona was concerned about
   - ☐ a. Felipe's health.
   - ☐ b. the Señora's health.
   - ☐ c. both a and b.

7. The Señora did not like
   - ☐ a. people to do her favors.
   - ☐ b. the smell of musk.
   - ☐ c. walking on the veranda.

8. Ramona was
   - ☐ a. afraid of the Señora.
   - ☐ b. a professional nurse.
   - ☐ c. allergic to flowers.

9. The Señora can best be described as
   - ☐ a. calm and compassionate.
   - ☐ b. icy and dominating.
   - ☐ c. sensitive and easily hurt.

10. The Señora could not
    - ☐ a. stand the thought of losing her son.
    - ☐ b. face her true feelings about Ramona.
    - ☐ c. both a and b.

from Narrative of the Life
of Frederick Douglass *by Frederick Douglass*

Long before daylight, I was called to go and rub, curry, and feed the horses. I obeyed, and was glad to obey. But whilst thus engaged, Mr. Covey entered the stable with a long rope. He caught hold of my legs, and was about tying me. As soon as I found what he was up to, I gave a sudden spring, and as I did so, he holding to my legs, I was brought sprawling on the stable floor. Mr. Covey seemed now to think he had me, and could do what he pleased. But at this moment—from whence came the spirit I don't know—I resolved to fight. I seized Covey hard by the throat; and as I did so, I rose. He held on to me, and I to him. My resistance was so entirely unexpected, that Covey seemed taken all aback. He trembled like a leaf. This gave me assurance, and I held him uneasy, causing the blood to run where I touched him with the end of my fingers. Mr. Covey soon called out to Hughes for help. Hughes came, and, while Covey held me, attempted to tie my right hand. While he was in the act of doing so, I watched my chance, and gave him a heavy kick close under the ribs. This kick fairly sickened Hughes, so that he left me in the hands of Mr. Covey. This kick had the effect of not only weakening Hughes, but Covey also. When he saw Hughes bending over with pain, his courage quailed. He asked me if I meant to persist in my resistance. I told him I did, come what might; that he had used me like a brute for six months, and that I was determined to be used so no longer. With that, he strove to drag me to a stick that was lying just out of the stable door. He meant to knock me down. But just as he was leaning over to get the stick, I seized him with both hands by his collar, and brought him by a sudden snatch to the ground. By this time, Bill came. Covey called upon him for assistance. Bill wanted to know what he could do. Covey said, "Take hold of him, take hold of him!" Bill said his master hired him out to work, and not to help whip me.

Recalling Facts

1. The narrator's job on this morning was to
   - ☐ a. pick cotton.
   - ☐ b. tend the horses.
   - ☐ c. paint the stable.

2. Mr. Covey tried to
   - ☐ a. shout a warning to the narrator.
   - ☐ b. shoot the narrator.
   - ☐ c. tie a rope around the narrator.

3. The narrator grabbed Mr. Covey by the
   - ☐ a. arm.
   - ☐ b. leg.
   - ☐ c. throat.

4. Mr. Covey cried out to Hughes
   - ☐ a. for help.
   - ☐ b. to run away.
   - ☐ c. to get his gun.

5. Bill
   - ☐ a. helped Mr. Covey.
   - ☐ b. didn't know Mr. Covey.
   - ☐ c. refused to help Mr. Covey.

Understanding the Passage

6. Mr. Covey apparently wanted to
   - ☐ a. punish the narrator.
   - ☐ b. have fun with the narrator.
   - ☐ c. talk to the narrator.

7. The narrator's resistance
   - ☐ a. made Mr. Covey happy.
   - ☐ b. surprised Mr. Covey.
   - ☐ c. was typical of his behavior.

8. The narrator's kick
   - ☐ a. disabled Hughes.
   - ☐ b. greatly helped Mr. Covey.
   - ☐ c. ended the fight.

9. The narrator
   - ☐ a. wanted the fight to end.
   - ☐ b. feared the consequences of the fight.
   - ☐ c. attempted to protect himself.

10. The narrator apparently was
    - ☐ a. handicapped.
    - ☐ b. very old.
    - ☐ c. very strong.

from **The Moonstone** *by Wilkie Collins*

About half-past seven in the morning I woke, and opened my window on a fine sunshiny day. The clock had struck eight, and I was just going out to chain up the dogs again, when I heard a sudden whisking of petticoats on the stairs behind me.

I quickly turned around. There was Penelope flying down after me like mad. "Father!" she screamed, "come up stairs, for God's sake! *The Diamond is gone!*"

Are you out of your mind?" I asked her.

"Gone!" says Penelope. "Gone, nobody knows how! Come up and see for yourself."

She dragged me after her into her young lady's sitting room, which opened into her bedroom. There, on the threshold of her bedroom door, stood Miss Rachel. The poor girl was almost as white in the face as the white dressing gown that clothed her. There also stood the two doors of the Indian cabinet, wide open. One of the drawers inside was pulled out as far as it would go.

"Look!" says Penelope. "I myself saw Miss Rachel put the Diamond into that drawer last night."

I went to the cabinet. The drawer was empty.

"Is this true, miss?" I asked.

With a look that was not like herself, with a voice that was not like her own, Miss Rachel answered, as my daughter had answered:

"The Diamond is gone."

Having said those words, she withdrew into her bedroom, and shut and locked the door.

Before we knew which way to turn next my lady came in, hearing my voice in her daughter's sitting room, and wondering what had happened. The news of the loss of the Diamond seemed to petrify her. She went straight to Miss Rachel's bedroom and insisted on being admitted. Miss Rachel let her in.

The alarm, running through the house like fire, caught the two gentlemen next.

Mr. Godfrey was the first to come out of his room. All he did when he heard what had happened was to hold up his hands in a state of bewilderment. This didn't say much for his natural strength of mind. Mr. Franklin, whose clear head I had confidently counted on to advise us, seemed to be as helpless as his cousin when he heard the news in his turn. For a wonder, he had had a good night's rest at last. The unaccustomed luxury of sleep had, as he said, apparently stupified him.

Recalling Facts

1. At eight o'clock in the morning Penelope's father
   - ☐ a. woke up.
   - ☐ b. charged into Penelope's bedroom.
   - ☐ c. was about to chain up the dogs.

2. The Diamond was put away by
   - ☐ a. Mr. Godfrey.
   - ☐ b. Penelope.
   - ☐ c. Miss Rachel.

3. The diamond had been stored in a
   - ☐ a. safe.
   - ☐ b. cabinet drawer.
   - ☐ c. desk drawer.

4. After going into her room, Miss Rachel
   - ☐ a. opened a window.
   - ☐ b. locked the door.
   - ☐ c. cried on her bed.

5. Mr. Godfrey and Mr. Franklin were
   - ☐ a. detectives.
   - ☐ b. cousins.
   - ☐ c. schoolteachers.

Understanding the Passage

6. Penelope's father's first reaction to the news of the missing diamond was
   - ☐ a. disbelief.
   - ☐ b. anger.
   - ☐ c. relief.

7. Miss Rachel appeared to be
   - ☐ a. in a state of shock.
   - ☐ b. hiding something.
   - ☐ c. anxious to talk to people.

8. Penelope's father
   - ☐ a. wanted to call the police.
   - ☐ b. knew Miss Rachel was not telling the truth.
   - ☐ c. appeared uncertain about what to do.

9. The news about the diamond
   - ☐ a. was hushed up.
   - ☐ b. spread quickly.
   - ☐ c. affected only Penelope.

10. Mr. Godfrey and Mr. Franklin
    - ☐ a. were of little help.
    - ☐ b. sprang into action.
    - ☐ c. went about their daily routine.

from **The Rocking-Horse Winner** *by D. H. Lawrence*

The family consisted of a mother, a father, a boy, and two little girls. They lived in a nice house with a garden. They had discreet servants and felt themselves superior to anyone in the neighborhood.

Although they lived in style, they felt always an anxiety in the house. There was never enough money. The mother had a small income, and the father had a small income, but not nearly enough for the social position which they had to keep up. The father went into town to some office. But though he had good prospects, these prospects never came to a thing. There was always the grinding sense of the shortage of money, though the style was always kept up.

At last the mother said, "I will see if *I* can't make something." But she did not know where to begin. She racked her brains. She tried this thing and the other, but could not find anything successful. The failure made deep lines come into her face. Her children were growing up. They would have to go to school. There must be more money, there must be more money. The father, who was always very handsome and expensive in his tastes, seemed as if he never *would* be able to do anything worth doing. And the mother, who had a great belief in herself, did not succeed any better, and her tastes were just as expensive.

And so the house came to be haunted by the unspoken phrase: *There must be more money! There must be more money!* The children could hear it all the time, though nobody said it aloud. They heard it at Christmas, when the expensive and splendid toys filled the nursery. Behind the shining modern rocking horse, behind the smart dollhouse, a voice would start whispering: "There *must* be more money! There *must* be more money!" And the children would stop playing, to listen for a moment. They would look into each other's eyes, to see if they had all heard. And each one saw in the eyes of the other two that they too had heard. "There *must* be more money! There *must* be more money!"

Yet nobody ever said it aloud. The whisper was everywhere, and therefore no one spoke it. Just as no one ever says: "We are breathing!" in spite of the fact that breath is coming and going all the time.

Recalling Facts

1. The family lived in a house with
   - ☐ a. a garden.
   - ☐ b. two other families.
   - ☐ c. red shutters.

2. The father had
   - ☐ a. no income.
   - ☐ b. a small income.
   - ☐ c. a large income.

3. The mother had
   - ☐ a. inherited a large sum of money.
   - ☐ b. no love for material objects.
   - ☐ c. expensive tastes.

4. The house was always filled with
   - ☐ a. friends.
   - ☐ b. music.
   - ☐ c. anxiety.

5. The mother's attempts to make extra money
   - ☐ a. angered the father.
   - ☐ b. doubled their savings.
   - ☐ c. did not succeed.

Understanding the Passage

6. The parents insisted on
   - ☐ a. keeping up the appearance of wealth.
   - ☐ b. sending their children to live with their grandparents.
   - ☐ c. putting their children to work.

7. At Christmastime, the children received
   - ☐ a. no presents.
   - ☐ b. a few inexpensive presents.
   - ☐ c. beautiful and expensive presents.

8. The phrase "There *must* be more money!" was heard
   - ☐ a. by no one.
   - ☐ b. only by the boy.
   - ☐ c. by the entire family.

9. The mother had no idea
   - ☐ a. how to make extra money.
   - ☐ b. where the father worked.
   - ☐ c. why her children were always crying.

10. The father was not
    - ☐ a. well educated.
    - ☐ b. concerned about what other people thought.
    - ☐ c. very successful in his job.

Johnsy's eyes were wide open as she looked out the window and counted—counted backward.

"Twelve," she said, and a little later "eleven"; and then "ten," and "nine"; and then "eight" and "seven," almost together.

Sue looked solicitously out of the window. What was there to count? There was only a bare dreary yard to be seen, and the blank side of the brick house twenty feet away. An old, old ivy vine, gnarled and decayed at the roots, climbed halfway up the brick wall. The cold breath of autumn had stricken the leaves from the vine until its skeleton branches clung, almost bare, to the crumbling bricks.

"What is it, dear?" asked Sue.

"Six," said Johnsy, in almost a whisper; "they're falling faster now. Three days ago there were almost a hundred. It made my head ache to count them; but now it's easy. There goes another one; there are only five left now."

"Five what, dear? Tell your Sudie."

"Leaves. On the ivy vine. When the last one falls I must go, too. I've known that for three days. Didn't the doctor tell you?"

"Oh, I never heard of such nonsense," complained Sue, with magnificent scorn. "What have old ivy leaves to do with your getting well? And you used to love that vine so, you naughty girl. Don't be a goosey. Why, the doctor told me this morning that your chances for getting well real soon were—let's see exactly what he said—he said the chances were ten to one! Why, that's almost as good a chance as we have in New York when we ride on the streetcars or walk past a new building. Try to take some broth now, and let Sudie go back to her drawing, so she can sell the editor man with it, and buy port wine for her sick child, and pork chops for her greedy self."

"You needn't get any more wine," said Johnsy, keeping her eyes fixed out the window. "There goes another. No, I don't want any broth. That leaves just four. I want to see the last one fall before it gets dark; then I'll go, too."

"Johnsy, dear," said Sue, bending over her, "will you promise me to keep your eyes closed, and not look out the window until I am done working? I must hand those drawings in by tomorrow and I need the light."

Recalling Facts

1. Johnsy was counting
   - ☐ a. vines.
   - ☐ b. raindrops.
   - ☐ c. leaves.

2. This passage takes place during the
   - ☐ a. fall.
   - ☐ b. spring.
   - ☐ c. summer.

3. Sue thought Johnsy's counting was
   - ☐ a. interesting.
   - ☐ b. nonsense.
   - ☐ c. amusing.

4. Sue worked as
   - ☐ a. a writer.
   - ☐ b. an artist.
   - ☐ c. a nurse.

5. Johnsy said she didn't want any
   - ☐ a. broth.
   - ☐ b. wine.
   - ☐ c. both a and b.

Understanding the Passage

6. Sue found Johnsy's behavior
   - ☐ a. healthy.
   - ☐ b. strange.
   - ☐ c. typical.

7. Johnsy felt that she was about to
   - ☐ a. die.
   - ☐ b. get well.
   - ☐ c. believe the doctor.

8. According to Sue, the doctor said that Johnsy's chances for recovery were
   - ☐ a. very good.
   - ☐ b. only fair.
   - ☐ c. poor.

9. Sue was anxious to
   - ☐ a. join in the counting.
   - ☐ b. shop for wine and food.
   - ☐ c. get back to her work.

10. Johnsy was anxious to
    - ☐ a. eat her supper.
    - ☐ b. see the last leaf fall.
    - ☐ c. get some sleep.

The place was as much of a wilderness as the densest wood, and there sat a duck on her nest; she was busy hatching her ducklings, but she was almost tired of it, because sitting is such a tedious business, and she had very few callers. The other ducks thought it more fun to swim about in the moat than to come and have a gossip with her under a wild rhubarb leaf.

At last one eggshell after another began to crack open. "Cheep, cheep!" All the yolks had come to life and were sticking out their heads.

"Quack, quack," said the duck, and all her ducklings came scurrying out as fast as they could, looking about under the green leaves, and their mother let them look as much as they liked, because green is good for the eyes.

"How big the world is!" said all the ducklings, for they felt much more comfortable now than when they were lying in the egg.

"Do you imagine this is the whole of the world?" asked their mother. "It goes far beyond the other side of the garden, right into the Rector's field, but I've never been there yet. I hope you're all here," she went on, and hoisted herself up. "No, I haven't got all of you even now; the biggest egg is still there. I wonder how much longer it will take! I'm getting rather bored with the whole thing." And she squatted down again on the nest.

"Well, how are you getting on?" asked an old duck who came to call on her.

"That last egg is taking an awfully long time," said the brooding duck. "It won't break; but let me show you the others, they're the sweetest ducklings I've ever seen. They are all exactly like their father; the scamp— he never comes to see me!"

"Let me look at the egg that won't break," said the old duck. "You may be sure it's a turkey's egg. I was fooled like that once, and the trouble and bother I had with those youngsters, because they were actually afraid of the water! I simply couldn't get them to go in! I quacked at them and I snapped at them, but it was no use. Let me see the egg—of course it's a turkey's egg. Leave it alone, and teach the other children to swim."

Recalling Facts

1. The mother duck found sitting on her eggs to be
   - □ a. fun.
   - □ b. easy.
   - □ c. boring.

2. Other ducks
   - □ a. came to visit the mother duck often.
   - □ b. preferred to swim rather than visit the mother duck.
   - □ c. offered to sit on the eggs for the mother duck.

3. The mother duck thought a good color to look at was
   - □ a. red.
   - □ b. yellow.
   - □ c. green.

4. The last unhatched egg was the
   - □ a. smallest.
   - □ b. biggest.
   - □ c. weakest.

5. The old duck thought that the last egg was a
   - □ a. turkey's egg.
   - □ b. duck's egg.
   - □ c. chicken's egg.

Understanding the Passage

6. The young ducklings were
   - □ a. happy to be out of their shells.
   - □ b. blind at first.
   - □ c. anxious to run away.

7. The young ducklings thought that
   - □ a. they should go beyond the Rector's field.
   - □ b. the whole world consisted of what they could see.
   - □ c. the last egg would be the best.

8. The failure of the last egg to crack
   - □ a. delighted the mother duck.
   - □ b. frustrated the mother duck.
   - □ c. made the mother duck furious.

9. The mother duck was disappointed in
   - □ a. her ducklings.
   - □ b. the ducklings' father.
   - □ c. the old duck.

10. The most important skill for a young duckling to learn is
    - □ a. sitting on eggs.
    - □ b. swimming.
    - □ c. hiding from the Rector.

Priam Farll's eyes fell on the coffin of Henry Leek with its white cross. And there was the end of Priam Farll's self-control. A pang seized him, and an issuing sob nearly ripped him in two. It was a loud sob, undisguised and unashamed. Other sobs succeeded it. Priam Farll was in torture. The organist vaulted over his seat, shocked by the outrage. "You really mustn't make that noise," whispered the organist.

Priam Farll shook him off.

The organist was apparently at a loss what to do.

"Who is it?" whispered one of the young men.

"Don't know him from Adam!" said the organist with conviction, and then to Priam Farll: "Who are you? You've no right to be here. Who gave you permission to come up here?" The rending sobs continued to issue from the full-bodied man of fifty.

"It's perfectly absurd!" whispered the youngster who had whispered before.

"Here! They're waiting for you!" whispered the other young man excitedly to the organist.

"By—!" whispered the alarmed organist, not stopping to say by what, but leaping like an acrobat back to his seat. His fingers and boots were at work instantly, and as he played he turned his head and whispered: "Better fetch someone to give us a hand."

One of the young men crept quickly and creakingly down the stairs. Fortunately the organ and choristers were now combined to overcome the sobbing, and they succeeded. Presently a powerful arm, hidden under a black cassock, was laid on Priam's shoulder. He tried to free himself, but he could not. The cassock and the two young men thrust him downwards. They all descended together, partly walking and partly falling. And then a door was opened, and Priam found himself in the unroofed air of the cloisters, without his hat, and breathing in gasps. His captors were also breathing in gasps. They glared at him in triumphant menace, as though they had done something, which indeed they had, and as though they meant to do something more but could not quite decide what.

"Where's your ticket of admission?" demanded the cassock.

Priam fumbled for it, and could not find it.

"I must have lost it," he said weakly.

"What's your name?"

"Priam Farll," said Priam Farll, without thinking.

"Off his nut!" murmured one of the young men. "Come on, Stan. Don't let's miss that anthem, for this cuss."

Recalling Facts

1. On the coffin of Henry Leek was a
   - □ a. white cross.
   - □ b. flower arrangement.
   - □ c. bible.

2. After viewing Leek's coffin, Priam Farll
   - □ a. left quietly.
   - □ b. cried loudly.
   - □ c. prayed fervently.

3. Priam Farll's behavior offended the
   - □ a. minister.
   - □ b. widow.
   - □ c. organist.

4. Priam Farll was grabbed by
   - □ a. a policeman.
   - □ b. a powerful arm.
   - □ c. the organist.

5. Priam Farll had lost his
   - □ a. coat.
   - □ b. ticket.
   - □ c. glasses.

Understanding the Passage

6. The death of Henry Leek
   - □ a. had no significant effect on Priam Farll.
   - □ b. crushed Priam Farll.
   - □ c. left Priam Farll penniless.

7. The funeral was apparently
   - □ a. open to the public.
   - □ b. a private affair.
   - □ c. held at the graveyard.

8. To the organist, Priam Farll was
   - □ a. a familiar face.
   - □ b. an old enemy.
   - □ c. a total stranger.

9. Priam Farll
   - □ a. was tossed out of the funeral service.
   - □ b. sobbed through the entire funeral service.
   - □ c. threatened he would leave the funeral service.

10. Priam Farll's captors thought he was
    - □ a. extremely ill.
    - □ b. not completely sane.
    - □ c. likely to cause more trouble.

There were once a man and a woman who had an only child. They lived quite alone in a solitary valley. It came to pass that the mother once went into the woods to gather branches of fir. She took with her little Hans, who was just two years old. As it was springtime, and the child took pleasure in the many-colored flowers, she went still further onwards with him into the forest. Suddenly two robbers sprang out of the thicket. They seized the mother and child, and carried them far away into the black forest. The poor woman urgently begged the robbers to set her and her child free. But their hearts were made of stone. They would not listen to her prayers and drove her on farther by force. After they had worked their way through bushes and briars for about two miles, they came to a rock where there was a door, at which the robbers knocked and it opened at once. They had to go through a long dark passage. At last they came into a great cavern which was lighted by a fire which burnt on the hearth. On the wall hung swords, sabers, and other deadly weapons which gleamed in the light. In the midst stood a black table at which four other robbers were sitting gambling. The captain sat at the head of it. As soon as he saw the woman he came and spoke to her, and told her to be at ease and have no fear, they would do nothing to hurt her, but she must look after the housekeeping. If she kept everything in order, she should not fare ill with them. Thereupon they gave her something to eat. They showed her a bed where she might sleep with her child.

The woman stayed many years with the robbers, and Hans grew tall and strong. His mother told him stories, and taught him to read an old book of tales about knights which she found in the cave. When Hans was nine years old, he made himself a strong club out of a branch of fir, hid it behind the bed, and then went to his mother and said, "Dear mother, pray tell me who is my father. I must and will know." His mother was silent and would not tell him, that he might not become homesick.

Recalling Facts

1. Hans and his parents lived
   - ☐ a. on top of a mountain.
   - ☐ b. alone in a valley.
   - ☐ c. in a small town.

2. Hans and his mother went into the woods to
   - ☐ a. hunt for deer.
   - ☐ b. pick blueberries.
   - ☐ c. gather branches.

3. Hans and his mother were attacked by
   - ☐ a. two robbers.
   - ☐ b. four robbers.
   - ☐ c. six robbers.

4. The captain of the robbers wanted Hans's mother to
   - ☐ a. do the housekeeping.
   - ☐ b. chop firewood.
   - ☐ c. leave Hans with them.

5. Hans's mother taught him to read stories about
   - ☐ a. robbers.
   - ☐ b. heroes.
   - ☐ c. knights.

Understanding the Passage

6. The mother went further into the forest to
   - ☐ a. please her son.
   - ☐ b. build a hut.
   - ☐ c. visit with neighbors.

7. The robbers who kidnapped the mother and her son were
   - ☐ a. friendly and kindhearted.
   - ☐ b. interested only in money.
   - ☐ c. cruel and coldhearted.

8. The robbers who kidnapped the mother and her son appeared to be
   - ☐ a. part of a larger gang.
   - ☐ b. very familiar with the forest.
   - ☐ c. both a and b.

9. The captain wanted to
   - ☐ a. ignore his captives.
   - ☐ b. punish his captives.
   - ☐ c. treat his captives fairly.

10. Apparently, Hans did not remember
    - ☐ a. his father.
    - ☐ b. his mother.
    - ☐ c. his age.

Smith locked up his room. He then went home for the first time in two months, telephoned for a stateroom on the Western Limited, and sent for Kerns, who arrived in an electric cab.

"I'm going to Illinois," said Smith, "tonight."

"The nation must know of this," said Kerns. "Let me wire ahead for fireworks."

"There'll be fireworks," observed Smith—"fireworks to burn. I'm going to get married to a working girl."

"Oh, piffle!" said Kerns faintly. "Let's go and sit on the third rail and talk it over."

"Not with *you*, idiot. Did you ever hear of Stanley Stevens, who tried to corner wheat? I think it's his daughter I'm going to marry. I'm going to Chicago to find out. Good heavens, Kerns! It's the most pitiful case, whoever she is! It's a case to stir the manhood of any man. I tell you it's got to be righted. I am thoroughly stirred up, and I won't stand any nonsense from you."

Kerns looked at him. "Smith," he pleaded in grave tones; "Smithy! For the sake of decency and of common sense—"

"Exactly," nodded Smith, picking up his hat and gloves; "for the sake of decency and of common sense. Good-bye Tommy. And—ah!"—pointing to a parcel of papers on the desk—"just have an architect look over these sketches with a view to estimating the—ah—cost of construction. And find some good landscape gardener to figure up what it will cost to remove a big ailantus tree from New York to the Berkshires. You can tell him I'll sue him if he injures the tree. But I don't care what it costs to move it."

"Smith!" faltered Kerns, "you're as mad as Hamlet!"

"It's one of my goals to be madder," retorted Smith, going out and running nimbly downstairs.

"Help!" observed Kerns feebly as the front door slammed. And, as nobody responded, he sat down in the bachelor quarters of J. Abingdon Smith, a prey to melancholy amazement.

When Smith had been gone a week Kerns wrote him. When he had been gone two weeks he telegraphed him. When the third week ended he telephoned him. And when the month was up he prepared to leave for darkest Chicago. In fact he was actually leaving his house, suitcase in hand, when Smith drove up in a hansom and gleefully waved his hand.

Recalling Facts

1. Smith told Kerns he was planning to travel to
   - ☐ a. Indiana.
   - ☐ b. Illinois.
   - ☐ c. Iowa.

2. Smith said he was going to marry a
   - ☐ a. working girl.
   - ☐ b. rich girl.
   - ☐ c. farm girl.

3. Stanley Stevens tried to corner the market in
   - ☐ a. gold.
   - ☐ b. construction materials.
   - ☐ c. wheat.

4. Smith wanted someone to move a
   - ☐ a. stateroom.
   - ☐ b. particular tree.
   - ☐ c. group of animals.

5. After Smith had been gone for a month, Kerns
   - ☐ a. wrote him.
   - ☐ b. telegraphed him.
   - ☐ c. prepared to leave for Chicago.

Understanding the Passage

6. Smith appeared to
   - ☐ a. have enough money to do what he wished.
   - ☐ b. be afraid to travel too far from home.
   - ☐ c. be in need of an expert lawyer.

7. Smith was
   - ☐ a. not willing to travel on a train.
   - ☐ b. not very familiar with his future bride's family.
   - ☐ c. a man lacking in decency and common sense.

8. Kerns appeared to
   - ☐ a. be afraid of Smith.
   - ☐ b. dislike Smith.
   - ☐ c. know Smith quite well.

9. Smith felt very strongly about
   - ☐ a. saving a lot of money.
   - ☐ b. staying in New York.
   - ☐ c. moving the ailantus tree.

10. Smith's marriage plans
    - ☐ a. delighted Kerns.
    - ☐ b. surprised Kerns.
    - ☐ c. were delayed by Kerns.

from **Life in the Iron Mills** *by Rebecca Harding Davis*

It was market day. The narrow window of the jail looked down directly on the carts and wagons drawn up in a long line, where they had unloaded. Hugh could see, too, and hear distinctly the clink of money as it changed hands, and busy crowd shoving, pushing one another, and swearing at the stalls. Somehow, the sound, more than anything else had done, woke him up—made the whole real to him. He was done with the world and the business of it. He looked out, pressing his face close to the rusty bars. How they crowded and pushed! And he—he should never walk ● that pavement again! There came Neff Sanders with a basket on his arm. Sure enough, Neff was married the other week. He whistled, hoping he would look up; but he did not. He wondered if Neff remembered he was there—if any of the boys thought of him up there, and thought that he never was to go down that old cinder road again. Never again! He had not quite understood it before; but now he did. Not for days or years, but never!—that was it.

How clear the light fell on that stall in front of the market! How like a ● picture it was, the dark green heaps of corn, and the crimson beets, and golden melons! There was another with game: how the light flickered on that pheasant's breast, with the purplish blood dripping over the brown feathers! He could see the red shining of the drops, it was so near. In one minute he could be down there. It was just a step. So easy, as it seemed, so natural to go! Yet it could never be—not in all the thousands of years to come—that he should put his foot on that street again! He tried to put ● the thought away, but it would come back. He, what had he done to bear this?

Then came the sudden picture of what might have been, and now. He knew what it was to be in the penitentiary—how it went with men there. He knew how in these long years he should slowly die, but not until soul and body had become corrupt and rotten—how, when he came out, if he lived to come, even the lowest mill hands would jeer him—how his hands would be weak, and his brain senseless and stupid.

Recalling Facts

1. Hugh's window looked out over
   - ☐ a. a school yard.
   - ☐ b. the marketplace.
   - ☐ c. the warden's home.

2. Neff Sanders had recently been
   - ☐ a. arrested.
   - ☐ b. married.
   - ☐ c. in to visit Hugh.

3. Neff came to market carrying a
   - ☐ a. pheasant.
   - ☐ b. barrel of corn.
   - ☐ c. basket.

4. To get Neff's attention, Hugh
   - ☐ a. banged on the bars.
   - ☐ b. whistled.
   - ☐ c. called him.

5. Hugh believed that in prison his hands would
   - ☐ a. be broken.
   - ☐ b. develop calluses.
   - ☐ c. become weak.

Understanding the Passage

6. Apparently, Hugh had been sentenced to
   - ☐ a. a few months in jail.
   - ☐ b. three years in jail.
   - ☐ c. many years in jail.

7. The sounds of the marketplace made Hugh realize
   - ☐ a. how much people missed him.
   - ☐ b. how sad his situation really was.
   - ☐ c. that prison was not such a bad place.

8. Hugh had not been
   - ☐ a. visited by Neff and the boys.
   - ☐ b. given any food.
   - ☐ c. able to write any letters.

9. Hugh longed to
   - ☐ a. talk to his family.
   - ☐ b. walk through the streets.
   - ☐ c. have a decent meal.

10. The penitentiary is a
   - ☐ a. depressing place.
   - ☐ b. temporary prison.
   - ☐ c. place for execution.

By nine o'clock all the people were in their berths. Annixter could hear one of the lady's children fidgeting and complaining. A stout gentleman snored monotonously. At intervals, a brakeman or the passenger conductor pushed down the aisle between the curtains, his red and white lamp over his arm. Looking out into the railroad car, Annixter saw in an end section, where the berths had not been made up, the porter in his white duck coat, dozing, his mouth open, his head on his shoulder.

The hours passed. Midnight came and went. Annixter, checking off the stations, noted their passage of Modesto, Merced, and Madeira. Then, after another broken nap, he lost count. He wondered where they were. Had they reached Fresno yet? Raising the window curtain, he made a shade with both hands on either side of his face and looked out. The night was thick, dark, clouded over. A fine rain was falling, leaving streaks on the glass of the outside window. Only the faintest gray blur indicated the sky.

"I think sure we must have passed Fresno," he muttered. He looked at his watch. It was about half-past three. "If we have passed Fresno," he said to himself, "I'd better wake the little girl pretty soon. She'll need about an hour to dress. Better find out for sure."

He drew on his trousers and shoes, got into his coat, and stepped out into the aisle. In the seat that had been occupied by the porter, the Pullman conductor, his cash box and car schedules before him, was checking up his berths, a blue pencil behind his ear.

"What's the next stop, captain?" inquired Annixter, coming up. "Have we reached Fresno yet?"

"Just passed it," the other responded, looking at Annixter over his spectacles.

"What's the next stop?"

"Goshen. We will be there in about forty-five minutes."

"Fair black night, isn't it?"

"Black as a pocket. Let's see, you're the party in upper and lower 9."

Annixter caught at the back of the nearest seat just in time to prevent a fall, and the conductor's cash box was shunted off the surface of the plush seat and came clanking to the floor. The lights overhead vibrated with blinding speed in the long, sliding jar that ran through the train from end to end, and the momentum of its speed suddenly decreasing, all but pitched the conductor from his seat.

Recalling Facts

1. The people slept in
   - ☐ a. hotel rooms.
   - ☐ b. their seats.
   - ☐ c. berths.

2. Modesto, Merced, and Madeira were
   - ☐ a. railroad trains.
   - ☐ b. train stations.
   - ☐ c. mountain passes.

3. The night was
   - ☐ a. rainy.
   - ☐ b. foggy.
   - ☐ c. clear.

4. The Pullman conductor said that the next stop was
   - ☐ a. Fresno.
   - ☐ b. Goshen.
   - ☐ c. Madeira.

5. The conductor was almost
   - ☐ a. pitched out of his seat.
   - ☐ b. thrown off the train.
   - ☐ c. hit with the cash box.

Understanding the Passage

6. Most of the passengers were
   - ☐ a. talking.
   - ☐ b. eating.
   - ☐ c. sleeping.

7. Annixter tried to keep a close watch on the
   - ☐ a. cash box.
   - ☐ b. train's progress.
   - ☐ c. Pullman conductor.

8. Annixter was traveling
   - ☐ a. by himself.
   - ☐ b. with a little girl.
   - ☐ c. with a large group of women.

9. The conductor apparently knew
   - ☐ a. Annixter's berth number.
   - ☐ b. the distance to Goshen.
   - ☐ c. both a and b.

10. The train
   - ☐ a. suddenly braked.
   - ☐ b. ran off the track.
   - ☐ c. increased its speed.

Tip was well soaked and dripping water. But he managed to lean forward and shout in the ear of the Saw-Horse: "Keep still, you fool! Keep still!" The horse at once ceased struggling and floated calmly upon the surface, its wooden body being as buoyant as a raft.

"What does the word 'fool' mean?" asked the horse.

"It is a term of reproach," answered Tip, somewhat ashamed of the expression. "I only use it when I am angry."

"Then it pleases me to be able to call you a fool, in return," said the horse. "For I did not make the river, nor put it in our way. So only a term of reproach is fit for one who becomes angry with me for falling into the water."

"That is quite evident," replied Tip; "So I am in the wrong." Then he called out to the Pumpkinhead: "are you all right, Jack?" There was no reply. So the boy called to the King: "are you all right, your majesty?"

The Scarecrow King groaned. "I'm all wrong, somehow," he said, in a weak voice. "How very wet this water is!"

Tip was bound so tightly by the cord that he could not turn his head to look at his companions. So he said to the Saw-Horse: "Paddle with your legs toward the shore." The horse obeyed. Although their progress was slow they finally reached the opposite river bank at a place where it was low enough to enable the creature to scramble upon dry land.

Tip managed to get his knife out of his pocket and cut the cords that bound the riders to one another and to the wooden horse. He heard the Scarecrow King fall to the ground with a mushy sound. Then Tip quickly dismounted and looked at his friend Jack.

The wooden body, with its gorgeous clothing, still sat upright upon the horse's back; but the pumpkin head was gone. Only the sharpened stick that served for a neck was visible. As for the Scarecrow King, the straw in his body had shaken down the jolting and packed itself into his legs and the lower part of his body—which appeared very plump and round while his upper half seemed like an empty sack. Upon his head the Scarecrow King still wore the heavy crown. It had been sewed on to prevent his losing it.

Recalling Facts

1. Tip called the Saw-Horse a
   - ☐ a. genius.
   - ☐ b. fool.
   - ☐ c. king.

2. Tip admitted to the Saw-Horse that he
   - ☐ a. was lost.
   - ☐ b. had no friends.
   - ☐ c. was in the wrong.

3. All the riders were
   - ☐ a. dry.
   - ☐ b. tied together.
   - ☐ c. good swimmers.

4. In his pocket, Tip had a
   - ☐ a. knife.
   - ☐ b. watch.
   - ☐ c. wallet.

5. The Scarecrow King wore a
   - ☐ a. funny hat.
   - ☐ b. pumpkin.
   - ☐ c. heavy crown.

Understanding the Passage

6. Apparently the characters came close to
   - ☐ a. drowning.
   - ☐ b. floating upriver.
   - ☐ c. tying up the Saw-Horse.

7. The Saw-Horse did not
   - ☐ a. speak English.
   - ☐ b. understand some words.
   - ☐ c. have a wooden body.

8. Tip, Jack, and the Scarecrow King crossed the river
   - ☐ a. in a boat.
   - ☐ b. on the Saw-Horse.
   - ☐ c. one at a time.

9. Jack lost his head
   - ☐ a. during the crossing.
   - ☐ b. after he was untied.
   - ☐ c. before entering the water.

10. The Scarecrow King
    - ☐ a. stayed dry.
    - ☐ b. lost his crown.
    - ☐ c. was soaking wet.

"Which man?" I cried, and then my eye caught the figure at which Basil Grant's bull's eyes were glaring.

"What has he done?" I asked.

"I am not sure of the details," said Grant, "but his sin is a desire to intrigue to the disadvantage of others. Probably he has adopted some act or other to effect his plan."

"What plan?" I asked. "If you know all about him why don't you tell me why he is the wickedest man in England? What is his name?"

Basil Grant stared at me for some moments.

"I think you've made a mistake in my meaning," he said. "I don't know his name. I never saw him before in my life."

"Never saw him before!" I cried, with a kind of anger. "Then what in Heaven's name do you mean by saying that he is the wickedest man in England?"

"I meant what I said," said Basil Grant, calmly. "The moment I saw that man, I saw all these people stricken with a sudden innocence. I saw that while all ordinary poor men in these streets were being themselves, he was not being himself. I saw that all the men in these slums—cadgers, pickpockets, hooligans—are all, in the deepest sense, trying to be good. And I saw that that man was trying to be evil."

"But if you never saw him before—" I began.

"In God's name, look at his face," cried out Basil, in a voice that startled the driver. "Look at the eyebrows. They mean that infernal pride which made Satan so proud that he sneered even at heaven when he was one of the first angels in it. Look at his mustaches! They are so grown as to insult humanity. In the name of the sacred heavens, look at his hair. In the name of God and the stars, look at his hat."

I stirred uncomfortably.

"But after all," I said, "this is very fanciful—perfectly absurd. Look at the mere facts. You have never seen the man before, you—"

"Oh, the mere facts," he cried out, in a kind of despair. "The mere facts! Do you really admit—are you still so sunk in superstitions, so clinging to dim and prehistoric altars, that you believe in facts? Do you not trust an immediate impression?"

"Well, an immediate impression may be," I said, "a little less practical than facts."

Recalling Facts

1. Basil Grant did not know the man's
   - ☐ a. name.
   - ☐ b. plan.
   - ☐ c. both a and b.

2. Basil called the man the wickedest man in
   - ☐ a. New England.
   - ☐ b. England.
   - ☐ c. Ireland.

3. Basil said that most men in the slums were trying to be
   - ☐ a. good.
   - ☐ b. happy.
   - ☐ c. evil.

4. One of the man's features that caught Basil's eye was his
   - ☐ a. nose.
   - ☐ b. eyebrows.
   - ☐ c. forehead.

5. The narrator was most interested in
   - ☐ a. people's looks.
   - ☐ b. first impressions.
   - ☐ c. the facts.

Understanding the Passage

6. Basil appeared to be
   - ☐ a. uncertain.
   - ☐ b. confident.
   - ☐ c. cautious.

7. Basil obviously trusted his
   - ☐ a. research.
   - ☐ b. instincts.
   - ☐ c. education.

8. The man's evil nature was
   - ☐ a. not apparent to the narrator.
   - ☐ b. noticed by everyone except the narrator.
   - ☐ c. overlooked by Basil.

9. The narrator believed facts were
   - ☐ a. often misleading.
   - ☐ b. usually used to mask the truth.
   - ☐ c. more practical than impressions.

10. Basil's comments about the man were
    - ☐ a. baffling.
    - ☐ b. upsetting.
    - ☐ c. depressing.

When Clym Yeobright was not with Eustacia he was sitting slavishly over his books; when he was not reading he was meeting her. These meetings were carried on with the greatest secrecy.

One afternoon his mother came home from a morning visit to Thomasin. He could see from a disturbance in the lines of her face that something had happened.

"I have been told an incomprehensible thing," she said mournfully. "The captain has let out at the Woman that you and Eustacia Vye are engaged to be married."

"We are," said Clym. "But it may not be for a very long time."

"I should hardly think it *would* be for a very long time! You will take her to Paris, I assume?" She spoke with weary hopelessness.

"I am not going back to Paris."

"What will you do with a wife, then?"

"Keep a school in Budmouth, as I have told you."

"That's foolish! The place is overrun with schoolmasters. You have no special qualifications. What chance is there for you?"

"There is no chance of getting rich. But with my system of education, which is as new as it is true, I shall do a great deal of good to my fellow creatures."

"Dreams, dreams! If there was a system left to be invented they would have found it out at the universities long before this time."

"Never, mother. They cannot find it out, because their teachers don't come in contact with the class which demands such a system—that is, those who have had no preliminary training. My plan is one for instilling high knowledge into empty minds."

"I might have believed you if you had kept yourself free from entanglements; but this woman—if she had been a good girl it would have been bad enough; but being such a—"

"She is a good girl."

"So you think. A Corfu bandmaster's daughter! What has her life been? Her surname even is not her true one."

"She is Captain Vye's granddaughter, and her father merely took her mother's name. And she is a lady by instinct."

"They call him 'captain,' but anybody is captain."

"He was in the Royal Navy!"

"No doubt he has been to sea in some tub or other. Why doesn't he look after her? No lady would rove about the heath at all hours of the day and night as she does."

Recalling Facts

1. Clym was engaged to marry
   ☐ a. Thomasin.
   ☐ b. Miss Budmouth.
   ☐ c. Eustacia.

2. Clym admitted he had no chance of
   ☐ a. meeting Captain Vye.
   ☐ b. leaving Paris.
   ☐ c. getting rich.

3. Miss Vye was the daughter of a
   ☐ a. bandmaster.
   ☐ b. schoolmaster.
   ☐ c. circus master.

4. Eustacia was Captain Vye's
   ☐ a. daughter.
   ☐ b. granddaughter.
   ☐ c. sister.

5. Captain Vye had spent some time in
   ☐ a. prison.
   ☐ b. the Royal Navy.
   ☐ c. America.

Understanding the Passage

6. Clym's mother did not
   ☐ a. approve of her son's engagement.
   ☐ b. know what Thomasin looked like.
   ☐ c. believe in education.

7. Clym believed Eustacia was
   ☐ a. a troublemaker.
   ☐ b. a fine woman.
   ☐ c. terribly ignorant.

8. Clym had
   ☐ a. special qualifications to become a teacher.
   ☐ b. great faith in his system of education.
   ☐ c. never completed high school.

9. Clym's mother did not think very highly of
   ☐ a. Eustacia.
   ☐ b. Captain Vye.
   ☐ c. both a and b.

10. Clym's mother could best be described as
    ☐ a. highly critical.
    ☐ b. generous.
    ☐ c. easily confused.

I thanked my uncle by clasping my hands. My heart was too full to speak.

"Yes," said he, "one more mouthful of water, the very last—do you hear, my boy?—the very last! I have taken care of it at the bottom of my bottle as the apple of my eye. Twenty times, a hundred times, I have resisted the desire to drink it. But—no—no, Harry, I have saved it for you."

"My dear uncle," I exclaimed, and the big tears rolled down my hot cheeks.

"Yes, my poor boy, I knew that when you reached this place, this cross-road in the earth, you would fall down half dead. I saved my last drop of water in order to restore you."

"Thanks," I cried; "thanks from my heart." I had recovered some of my strength. "Well," I said, "there can be no doubt now as to what we have to do. Our journey is at an end. Let us return."

While I spoke thus, my uncle avoided my face: he held down his head; his eyes were turned in every direction but the right one.

"Yes," I continued, getting excited by my own words, "we must go back to Sneffels. May Heaven give us strength to enable us once more to revisit the light of day. Would that we now stood on the summit of that crater."

"Go back," said my uncle, speaking to himself—"and must it be so?"

"Go back—yes, and without losing a single moment," I cried. For some moments there was silence under that dark and gloomy vault.

"So, my dear Harry," said my uncle the Professor, in a very singular tone of voice, "those few drops of water have not sufficed to restore your courage."

"Courage!" I cried.

"I see that you are quite as downcast as before, and still give way to despair."

What, then, was the man made of, and what other projects were entering his fertile brain?

"You are not discouraged, sir?"

"What! Give up just as we are on the verge of success?" he cried. "Never, never shall it be said that Professor Hardwigg retreated."

"Then we must make up our minds to perish," I cried, with a helpless sigh.

"No, Harry, my boy; certainly not. Go, leave me; I am very far from desiring your death. Take Hans with you. *I will go on alone.*"

Recalling Facts

1. The uncle gave Harry
   - ☐ a. a bandage.
   - ☐ b. a piece of an apple.
   - ☐ c. the last drops of water.

2. Harry wanted to
   - ☐ a. return to Sneffels.
   - ☐ b. stay just where he was.
   - ☐ c. move on.

3. Harry wished that he was
   - ☐ a. on the summit of the crater.
   - ☐ b. in the center of the earth.
   - ☐ c. dead.

4. The uncle decided to
   - ☐ a. turn back.
   - ☐ b. make camp.
   - ☐ c. go on alone.

5. The Professor did not want
   - ☐ a. to continue the journey.
   - ☐ b. his nephew to die.
   - ☐ c. the journey to be a success.

Understanding the Passage

6. The uncle
   - ☐ a. wanted to drink the water.
   - ☐ b. felt responsible for Harry.
   - ☐ c. both a and b.

7. The uncle had expected
   - ☐ a. trouble at this place.
   - ☐ b. a smooth voyage.
   - ☐ c. that Harry would outlast him.

8. The uncle and Harry
   - ☐ a. shared the same enthusiasm.
   - ☐ b. had a disagreement.
   - ☐ c. didn't like each other.

9. Harry wanted to return
   - ☐ a. after resting a while.
   - ☐ b. only after reaching their goal.
   - ☐ c. immediately.

10. Harry was sure that following the Professor would mean
    - ☐ a. death.
    - ☐ b. success.
    - ☐ c. fame.

Cravatte's rebels desolated the country and the army was in vain placed on his track. In the midst of all this terror the Bishop arrived on his visitation, and the Mayor came to him and urged him to turn back. Cravatte held the mountain as far as Arche and beyond, and there was danger, even with an escort. It would be uselessly exposing three or four unhappy soldiers.

"For that reason," said the Bishop, "I will go without escort."

"Can you mean it, Monseigneur?" the Mayor exclaimed.

"I mean it so fully that I absolutely refuse the soldiers and intend to start within an hour."

"Monseigneur, you will not do that!"

"There is in the mountain," the Bishop continued, "a humble little parish, which I have not visited for three years. They are good friends of mine, and quiet and honest shepherds. They are the owners of one goat out of every thirty they guard; they make very pretty woolen robes of different colors, and they play mountain airs on small six-holed flutes. They want to hear about heaven every now and then, and what would they think of a bishop who was afraid? What would they say if I did not go?"

"But Monseigneur, the rebels."

"Ah," said the Bishop, "you are right; I may meet them. They too must want to hear about heaven."

"But this band is a flock of wolves."

"Monsieur Mayor, it may be that this is precisely the flock of which Christ has made me the shepherd. Who knows the ways of God?"

"Monseigneur, they will plunder you."

"I haven't anything for them to take."

"They will kill you."

"A poor old priest who passes by, muttering his prayers? Nonsense, what good would it do them to kill me?"

"Oh, good gracious, if you were to meet them!"

"I would ask them for alms for my poor."

"Monseigneur, do not go. You will be exposing your life."

"My good sir," said the Bishop, "is that all? I am not in this world to save my life, but to save souls."

There was no help for it; he set out accompanied only by a lad, who offered to act as his guide. His stubbornness created a stir in the country and caused considerable alarm. He crossed the mountain on a mule, met nobody, and reached his friends, the goatherds, safely.

Recalling Facts

1. Cravatte was the leader of the
   - ☐ a. church.
   - ☐ b. army.
   - ☐ c. rebels.

2. The Bishop refused
   - ☐ a. soldiers as an escort.
   - ☐ b. to visit the shepherds.
   - ☐ c. to travel alone.

3. The shepherds played music on
   - ☐ a. stringed instruments.
   - ☐ b. flutes.
   - ☐ c. horns.

4. The Mayor compared the rebels to a
   - ☐ a. band of thieves.
   - ☐ b. flock of wolves.
   - ☐ c. group of misguided pilgrims.

5. The Bishop's guide was
   - ☐ a. an old man.
   - ☐ b. a young lad.
   - ☐ c. a rebel leader.

Understanding the Passage

6. The Mayor was concerned about the Bishop's
   - ☐ a. sanity.
   - ☐ b. safety.
   - ☐ c. religious convictions.

7. The Bishop appeared to be
   - ☐ a. very religious.
   - ☐ b. quite fearful.
   - ☐ c. disappointed with the Mayor.

8 The shepherds
   - ☐ a. worked for other people.
   - ☐ b. lacked any religious faith.
   - ☐ c. were reserved and independent.

9. The Bishop felt that the rebels would
   - ☐ a. kill him.
   - ☐ b. show little interest in him.
   - ☐ c. join the shepherds in the field.

10. The Bishop was very clear about
   - ☐ a. how to find the shepherds.
   - ☐ b. his mission in life.
   - ☐ c. both a and b.

from **Peter and Wendy** *by James M. Barrie*

As the pirates advanced, the quick eye of Starkey sighted Nibs disappearing through the wood, and at once his pistol flashed out. But an iron claw gripped his shoulder.

"Captain, let go!" he cried, writhing.

Now for the first time we hear the voice of Hook. It was an evil voice. "Put back that pistol first," it said threateningly.

"It was one of those boys you hate. I could have shot him dead."

"Ay, and the sound would have brought Tiger Lily's Indians upon us. Do you want to lose your scalp?"

"Shall I go after him, captain," asked pathetic Smee, "and tickle him with Johnny Corkscrew?" Smee had names for everything. His cutlass was Johnny Corkscrew, because he wriggled it in the wound. One could mention many lovable traits in Smee. For instance, after killing, it was his spectacles he wiped instead of his weapon.

"Johnny's a silent fellow," he reminded Hook.

"Not now, Smee," Hook said darkly. "He is only one, and I want to mischief all the seven. Scatter and look for them."

The pirates disappeared among the trees, and in a moment their captain and Smee were alone. Hook heaved a heavy sigh, and I know not why it was; perhaps it was because of the soft beauty of the evening, but there came over him a desire to confide to his faithful bo'son his life story. He spoke long and earnestly, but what it was all about, Smee, who was rather stupid, did not know in the least.

Anon he caught the word Peter.

"Most of all," Hook was saying passionately, "I want their captain, Peter Pan. 'Twas he cut off my arm." He brandished the hook threateningly. "I've waited long to shake his hand with this. Oh, I'll tear him!"

"And yet," said Smee, "I have often heard you say that hook was worth a score of hands, for combing the hair and other homely uses."

"Ay," the captain answered, "if I was a mother I would pray to have my children born with this instead of that," and he cast a look of pride upon his iron hand and one of scorn upon the other. Then again he frowned.

"Peter flung my arm," he said, wincing, "to a crocodile that happened to be passing by."

"I have often," said Smee, "noticed your dread of crocodiles."

"Not of crocodiles," Hook corrected him, "but of that one crocodile."

Recalling Facts

1. Starkey wanted to
   - ☐ a. hang Nibs.
   - ☐ b. shoot Nibs.
   - ☐ c. stab Nibs.

2. Hook was afraid of arousing the
   - ☐ a. pirates.
   - ☐ b. boys.
   - ☐ c. Indians.

3. Johnny Corkscrew was a
   - ☐ a. cutlass.
   - ☐ b. pirate.
   - ☐ c. ship.

4. Hook told his life story to
   - ☐ a. Tiger Lily.
   - ☐ b. Smee.
   - ☐ c. Starkey.

5. Hook had a strange dread of
   - ☐ a. his iron hand.
   - ☐ b. anything in the water.
   - ☐ c. one particular crocodile.

Understanding the Passage

6. The pirates could best be described as
   - ☐ a. friendly.
   - ☐ b. bloodthirsty.
   - ☐ c. cowardly.

7. Hook appeared to be afraid of
   - ☐ a. the seven boys.
   - ☐ b. his own men.
   - ☐ c. the Indians.

8. Hook told his life story because
   - ☐ a. he was about to die.
   - ☐ b. the pirates asked him to.
   - ☐ c. he felt an urge to talk.

9. Hook's greatest desire was to
   - ☐ a. get revenge for his lost arm.
   - ☐ b. have children of his own.
   - ☐ c. find that one crocodile.

10. Hook felt his iron hand was
    - ☐ a. completely worthless.
    - ☐ b. more useful than his other hand.
    - ☐ c. no different from his other hand.

The leather holster on his belt was hard and stiff. He oiled it and worked it soft with strong hands. The little room, which had only one window, began to grow dark as the short afternoon waned.

It was still daylight, however, when Nevada went out, to walk leisurely down the road into town. He came at length to the narrow block where there were a few horses and vehicles along the hitching rails, and people passing to and fro. There were several stores and shops, a saloon, and a restaurant, that appeared precisely as they had always been. A Chinaman, standing in a doorway, stared keenly at Nevada. His black eyes showed recognition. Then Nevada arrived at a corner store, where he entered. The place had the smell of general merchandise, groceries, and tobacco combined. To Jones's credit, he had never sold liquor. There was a boy clerk waiting on a woman customer, and Jones, a long lanky Westerner, who had seen range days himself.

"Howdy, Mr. Jones!" said Nevada, stepping forward.

"Howdy yourself, stranger!" replied the storekeeper. "You got the best of me."

"Wal, it's a little dark in heah or your eyes are failin'," returned Nevada, with a grin. Whereupon the other took a stride and bent over to peer into Nevada's face.

"I'm a son of a gun," he declared. "Jim Lacy! Back in Lineville! I've seen fellers come back I liked less." He shook hands heartily with Nevada. "Where you been, boy? You sure look well an' fine to me."

"Oh, I've been all over, knockin' about, lookin' for a job," drawled Nevada, easily.

"An' you come back to Lineville in winter, lookin' for a job?" laughed Jones.

"Shore," drawled Nevada.

"Jim, I'll bet if I offered you work you'd shy like a colt. Fact is, though, I could do it. I'm not doin' so bad here. There's a lumber company cuttin' up in the foothills. It's a long haul to Salisbar, but they pass through here. Heard about Salisbar?"

"Yes. Reckon I'll have to take a look at it. How far away?"

"Eighty miles or so," returned Jones. "Some miners struck it rich, an' that started Salisbar off as a minin' town. But it's growin' otherwise. Besides mineral, there are timber an' water, some good farm land, an' miles of grazin'. All this is wakin' Lineville up. There's business goin' on an' more comin'."

Recalling Facts

1. The first building Nevada entered was a
   - □ a. saloon.
   - □ b. restaurant.
   - □ c. corner store.

2. Jones never sold
   - □ a. tobacco.
   - □ b. liquor.
   - □ c. rifles.

3. Nevada said he was looking for
   - □ a. the sheriff.
   - □ b. an old friend.
   - □ c. a job.

4. Salisbar was
   - □ a. a booming town.
   - □ b. a lumbering company.
   - □ c. the name of a mountain.

5. Salisbar was about
   - □ a. fifty miles away.
   - □ b. eighty miles away.
   - □ c. one hundred miles away.

Understanding the Passage

6. The leather holster
   - □ a. was very expensive.
   - □ b. had not been cared for recently.
   - □ c. was left in Nevada's room.

7. Apparently, Nevada had
   - □ a. never seen the town before.
   - □ b. lived in Lineville before.
   - □ c. just discovered gold in the foothills.

8. Nevada and Jones had been
   - □ a. enemies.
   - □ b. strangers.
   - □ c. on friendly terms.

9. The expression "you'd shy like a colt" meant that Nevada
   - □ a. was afraid of horses.
   - □ b. would not accept a job from Jones.
   - □ c. was looking for a gunfight.

10. Salisbar was growing
    - □ a. more slowly than Lineville.
    - □ b. more quickly than Lineville.
    - □ c. at the same rate as Lineville.

"It is most provoking," said the Baroness, as her guests sat round the fire; "all the time that she had been with us I cannot remember that she was ever seriously ill, too ill to go about and do her work, I mean. And now, when I have the house full, and she could be useful in so many ways, she goes and breaks down. One is sorry for her, of course. She looks so withered and shrunken. But it is intensely annoying all the same."

"Most annoying," agreed the banker's wife. "It is the intense cold, I expect, it breaks the old people up."

"The frost is the sharpest that has been known in December for many years," said the Baron.

"And, of course, she is quite old," said the Baroness. "I wish I had given her notice some weeks ago. Then she would have left before this happened to her. Why, Wappi, what's the matter with you?"

The small, woolly lapdog had leapt suddenly down from its cushion and crept shivering under the sofa. At the same moment an outburst of angry barking came from the dogs in the castle yard. Other dogs could be heard yapping and barking in the distance.

"What is disturbing the animals?" asked the Baron.

And then the humans, listening intently, heard the sound that had roused the dogs to their fear and rage.

"Wolves!" cried the Baron.

Their music broke forth in one raging burst, seeming to come from everywhere.

"Hundreds of wolves," said the Hamburg merchant.

Moved by some impulse which she could not have explained, the Baroness left her guests. She made her way to the narrow, cheerless room where the old governess lay. In spite of the biting cold of the winter night, the window stood open. The Baroness rushed forward to close it.

"Leave it open," said the old woman in a voice that for all its weakness carried an air of command such as the Baroness had never heard before from her lips.

"But you will die of cold!" she said.

"I am dying in any case," said the voice, "and I want to hear their music. They have come from far and wide to sing the death music of my family. It is beautiful that they have come. I am the last Von Cernogratz that will die in our old castle. They have come to sing to me."

Recalling Facts

1. The banker's wife thought that the governess was ill because
   - ☐ a. she was working too hard.
   - ☐ b. the weather was so cold.
   - ☐ c. she was trying to avoid work.

2. The events in this passage took place in the month of
   - ☐ a. July.
   - ☐ b. January.
   - ☐ c. December.

3. Wappi was the name of the
   - ☐ a. governess.
   - ☐ b. doctor.
   - ☐ c. lapdog.

4. The animals were disturbed by the
   - ☐ a. fierce storm.
   - ☐ b. party guests.
   - ☐ c. howling wolves.

5. The governess refused to
   - ☐ a. close the window.
   - ☐ b. get dressed.
   - ☐ c. talk to the Baroness.

Understanding the Passage

6. The governess's illness seemed to
   - ☐ a. annoy the Baroness.
   - ☐ b. sadden the Baroness.
   - ☐ c. relieve the Baroness.

7. The winter frost was
   - ☐ a. milder than usual.
   - ☐ b. about average.
   - ☐ c. sharper than usual.

8. Dogs react strongly when they hear
   - ☐ a. high whistles.
   - ☐ b. the cry of wolves.
   - ☐ c. mournful singing.

9. The Baroness
   - ☐ a. wanted to nurse the governess.
   - ☐ b. did not want the governess to get cold.
   - ☐ c. felt no need to see the governess.

10. The governess believed that the wolves had come to
    - ☐ a. torment her.
    - ☐ b. sing to her.
    - ☐ c. frighten the Baroness.

from **Marriage á la Mode** *by Katherine Mansfield*

On his way to the station Williams remembered with a fresh pang of dis-appointment that he was taking nothing down to the kiddies. Poor little chaps! It was hard on them. Their first words always were as they ran to greet him, "What have you got for me, daddy?" and he had nothing. He would have to buy them some sweets at the station. But that was what he had done for the past four Saturdays. Their faces had fallen last time when they saw the same old boxes again.

And Paddy had said, "I had red ribbing on mine *bee*-fore!"

And Johnny had said, "It's always pink on mine. I hate pink!"

But what was William to do? The affair wasn't so easily settled. In the old days, of course, he would have taken a taxi off to a decent toy shop and chosen them something in five minutes. But nowadays they had Russian toys, French toys, Serbian toys—toys from God knows where. It was over a year since Isabel had scrapped the old donkeys and engines and so on because they were "so bad for the babies' sense of form."

"It's so important," the new Isabel had explained, "that they should like the right things from the very beginning. It saves so much time later on. Really, if the poor pets have to spend their infant years staring at these horrors, they'll grow up asking to be taken to the Royal Academy."

And she spoke as though a visit to the Royal Academy was certain death to anyone.

"Well, I don't know," said William slowly. "When I was their age I used to go to bed hugging an old towel with a knot in it."

The new Isabel looked at him, her eyes narrowed, her lips apart.

"*Dear* William! I'm sure you did!" She laughed in the new way.

Sweets it would have to be, however, thought William gloomily. He fished in his pocket for change for the taximan. And he saw the kiddies handing the boxes round—they were awfully generous little chaps—while Isabel's precious friends didn't hesitate to help themselves.

What about fruit? William hovered before a stall just inside the station. What about a melon each? Would they have to share that, too? Or a pine-apple for Pad, and a melon for Johnny? Isabel's friends could hardly go sneaking up to the nursery at the children's mealtimes.

Recalling Facts

1. Paddy and Johnny were tired
   of receiving
   ☐ a. fruit.
   ☐ b. sweets.
   ☐ c. toys.

2. Johnny didn't like
   ☐ a. blue ribbing.
   ☐ b. red ribbing.
   ☐ c. pink ribbing.

3. Isabel had thrown out
   the boys'
   ☐ a. sweets and fruit.
   ☐ b. Russian and Serbian toys.
   ☐ c. old donkeys and engines.

4. When William was a boy, he
   went to bed with an old
   ☐ a. towel.
   ☐ b. donkey.
   ☐ c. train.

5. At the station, William
   considered buying the boys
   ☐ a. a ride in a taxicab.
   ☐ b. new sweaters.
   ☐ c. fruit.

Understanding the Passage

6. William did not want to
   disappoint
   ☐ a. Isabel's friends.
   ☐ b. Paddy and Johnny.
   ☐ c. the stationmaster.

7. In the old days, William
   ☐ a. never worked on a
       Saturday.
   ☐ b. didn't have money to
       buy presents.
   ☐ c. had no trouble picking
       out toys for his sons.

8. The new Isabel scorned
   ☐ a. fruits and vegetables.
   ☐ b. all foreign toys.
   ☐ c. the Royal Academy.

9. William thought Isabel's
   friends were
   ☐ a. cold and distant.
   ☐ b. simply delightful.
   ☐ c. a bit rude and greedy.

10. William wanted to buy the
    boys something they would
    ☐ a. use as adults.
    ☐ b. take to bed with them.
    ☐ c. not have to share with
        Isabel's friends.

His right name was Frank X. Farrell, and I guess the X stood for "Excuse me." Because he never pulled a play, good or bad, on or off the field, without apologizin' for it. "Alibi Ike" was the name Carey wished on him the first day he reported down South. O' course we all cut out the "Alibi" part of it right away for the fear he would overhear it and bust somebody. But we called him "Ike" right to his face and the rest of it was understood by everybody on the club except Ike himself.

He ast me one time, he says: "What do you all call me Ike for?"

"Carey give you the name," I says. "It's his nickname for everybody he takes a likin' to."

"He mustn't have only a few friends then," says Ike. "I never heard him say 'Ike' to nobody else."

But I was goin' to tell you about Carey namin' him. We'd been workin' out two weeks and the pitchers was showin' somethin' when this bird joined us. His first day out he stood up there so good and took such a reef at the old pill that he had everyone lookin'. Then him and Carey was together in left field, catchin' fungoes, and it was after we was through for the day that Carey told me about him. "What do you think of Alibi Ike?" ast Carey.

"Who's that?" I says.

"This here Farrell in the outfield," says Carey.

"He looks like he could hit," I says.

"Yes," said Carey, "but he can't hit near as good as he can apologize." Then Carey went on to tell me what Ike had been pullin' out there. He'd dropped the first fly ball that was hit to him and told Carey his glove wasn't broke in yet, and Carey says the glove could easy of been Kid Gleason's gran'father. He made a whale of a catch out o' the next one and Carey says "Nice work!" but Ike says he could of caught the ball with his back turned only he slipped when he started after it.

"I thought you done well to get to the ball," says Carey.

"I ought to been settin' under it," says Ike.

"What did you hit last year?" Carey ast him.

"I had malaria most o' the season," says Ike. "I wound up with 356."

"Where would I have to go to get malaria?" says Carey, but Ike didn't wise up.

I and Carey and him set at the same table together for supper. It took him half an hour longer'n us to eat because he had to excuse himself every time he lifted his fork.

Recalling Facts

1. Frank X. Farrell got his nickname from
   □ a. Kid Gleason.
   □ b. his grandfather.
   □ c. Carey.

2. Ike was constantly
   □ a. bragging.
   □ b. apologizing.
   □ c. criticizing.

3. Ike
   □ a. played the outfield.
   □ b. played the infield.
   □ c. was the team's catcher.

4. Ike said he hit only 356 because he
   □ a. had malaria.
   □ b. had a sore shoulder.
   □ c. was underweight.

5. At supper, Ike excused himself every time he
   □ a. dropped his napkin.
   □ b. spilled the sugar.
   □ c. lifted his fork.

Understanding the Passage

6. Other players dropped "Alibi" from Ike's name because
   □ a. they thought it would upset him.
   □ b. Carey would have been upset.
   □ c. other players were also called "Alibi."

7. The phrase "when this bird joined us" refers to
   □ a. Carey's joining the team.
   □ b. Ike's joining the team.
   □ c. Gleason's joining the team.

8. Carey
   □ a. had known Ike for several years.
   □ b. had heard of Ike before.
   □ c. had just met Ike.

9. As a fielder, Ike appeared to have
   □ a. a weak throwing arm.
   □ b. excellent speed.
   □ c. trouble with ground balls.

10. The other members of the team thought Ike was
    □ a. odd.
    □ b. rude.
    □ c. mean.

"I should like to commemorate your birthday," Paul said. He opened the case, and with its lifted lid he held it out to Jean. "It will give me great pleasure if you'll kindly accept this little ornament."

Jean took it from him—she seemed to study it a minute. "Oh, Paul, oh, Paul!"—her protest was as sparing as a caress with the back of the hand.

"I thought you might care for the stone," he said.

"It's a rare and perfect one—it's magnificent."

"Well, Miss Armiger told me you would know." There was a hint of relaxed suspense in Paul's tone.

Still holding the case open, his companion looked at him a moment. "Did *she* kindly select it?"

He stammered, coloring a little. "No; mother and I did. We went up to London for it; we had the mounting designed and worked out. They took two months. But I showed it to Miss Armiger, and she said you'd spot any defect."

"Do you mean," the girl asked, smiling, "that if you had not had her word for that, you would have tried me with something inferior?"

Paul continued very grave. "You know well enough what I mean."

Without again noticing the contents of the case she softly closed it and kept it in her hand. "Yes, Paul, I know well enough what you mean." She looked round her; then, as if her old familiarity with him were refreshed and sweetened: "Come and sit down with me." She led the way to a garden bench that stood at a distance from Mrs. Beever's tea table, an old green wooden bench that was a perennial feature of the spot. "If Miss Armiger knows that I'm a judge," she pursued as they went, "it's because, I think, she knows everything—everything except one thing, which I know better than she." She seated herself, glancing up and putting out her free hand to him with an air of comradeship and trust. Paul let it take his own, which it held there a minute. "I know *you*." She drew him down, and he dropped her hand; whereupon it returned to his little box, which, with the aid of the other, it tightly and nervously clasped. "I can't take your present. It's impossible."

He sat leaning forward with his big red fists on his knees. "Not for your birthday?"

"No, it's too splendid for that."

Recalling Facts

1. Paul gave Jean a present to celebrate
   - ☐ a. their engagement.
   - ☐ b. Jean's birthday.
   - ☐ c. the new year.

2. Jean asked if
   - ☐ a. Miss Armiger had picked out the stone.
   - ☐ b. Paul's mother knew about the present.
   - ☐ c. Paul would hold the case for her.

3. Paul got the stone
   - ☐ a. from Mrs. Beever.
   - ☐ b. from Miss Armiger.
   - ☐ c. in London.

4. Jean led Paul to a
   - ☐ a. small stream.
   - ☐ b. store window.
   - ☐ c. garden bench.

5. Jean said she could not
   - ☐ a. accept the present.
   - ☐ b. wait to leave for London.
   - ☐ c. both a and b.

Understanding the Passage

6. Paul's gift to Jean was
   - ☐ a. an expensive piece of jewelry.
   - ☐ b. a poor-quality trinket.
   - ☐ c. a handmade jewelry box.

7. Jean thought the present was
   - ☐ a. a cheap imitation.
   - ☐ b. the wrong size.
   - ☐ c. beautiful.

8. Miss Armiger thought Jean had a lot of
   - ☐ a. nerve to ask for a birthday present.
   - ☐ b. knowledge about precious stones.
   - ☐ c. earrings she never wore.

9. Jean believed she knew Paul
   - ☐ a. very well.
   - ☐ b. only casually.
   - ☐ c. almost as well as Miss Armiger did.

10. Jean did not want to keep the present because she thought
   - ☐ a. Paul didn't really love her.
   - ☐ b. it was too extravagant.
   - ☐ c. Miss Armiger had picked it out.

31 *from* **Victory** *by Joseph Conrad*

Heyst and Lena, walking rather fast, approached Wang's hut. He asked the girl to wait. Then Heyst climbed the ladder of bamboos giving access to the door. It was as he had thought. The smoky room was empty, except for a big chest of sandalwood too heavy for hurried removal. Its lid was thrown up. But whatever it might have contained was no longer there. All Wang's things were gone. Without tarrying in the hut, Heyst came back to the girl, who asked no questions, with her strange air of knowing everything.

"Let us push on," he said.

He went ahead, the rustle of her white skirt following him into the shades of the forest, along the path of their usual walk. Twice Heyst looked over his shoulder at her. Behind the readiness of her smile there was a fund of devoted love. They passed the spot where it was their practice to turn towards the barren summit of the central hill. Heyst held steadily on his way towards the upper limit of the forest. The moment they left its shelter, a breeze enveloped them. A great cloud, racing over the sun, threw a somber tint over everything. Heyst pointed up a steep rugged path clinging to the side of the hill. It ended in a barricade of felled trees, a primitive obstacle which must have cost much labor to erect at just that spot.

"This," Heyst explained in his urbane tone, "is a barrier against the march of progress. The poor folk over there did not like it. It appeared to them in the shape of my company—a great step forward, as some people used to call it with mistaken faith. The advanced foot has been drawn back, but the barricade remains."

They went on climbing slowly. The cloud had driven over, leaving an added brightness on the face of the world.

"It's a very ridiculous thing," Heyst went on; "but then it is the product of honest fear—fear of the unknown. It's pathetic, too, in a way. And I wish, Lena, that we were on the other side of it."

"Oh, stop, stop!" she cried, seizing his arm.

The face of the barricade they were approaching had been piled up with a lot of fresh-cut branches. The leaves were still green.

"You had better let me go forward alone, Lena," said Heyst.

Recalling Facts

1. Wang's hut was empty except for a
   - ☐ a. big chest.
   - ☐ b. mirror.
   - ☐ c. bed.

2. When Heyst returned from the hut, Lena
   - ☐ a. urged him to push on.
   - ☐ b. asked no questions.
   - ☐ c. wanted to know what he had found.

3. Lena was wearing
   - ☐ a. jungle clothes.
   - ☐ b. a white skirt.
   - ☐ c. high-heeled shoes.

4. The path Heyst and Lena traveled was
   - ☐ a. flat and broad.
   - ☐ b. muddy and dangerous.
   - ☐ c. steep and rugged.

5. The path ended
   - ☐ a. at a cliff.
   - ☐ b. in a barricade of trees.
   - ☐ c. at the river's edge.

Understanding the Passage

6. When Heyst looked inside Wang's hut, he was
   - ☐ a. not surprised.
   - ☐ b. very irritated.
   - ☐ c. intensely shocked.

7. Apparently, Wang
   - ☐ a. had been planning to leave.
   - ☐ b. had left in a hurry.
   - ☐ c. would be right back.

8. The summit of the central hill was
   - ☐ a. heavily populated.
   - ☐ b. covered with jungle growth.
   - ☐ c. without many trees or vegetation.

9. The barricade was a protest against
   - ☐ a. poor living conditions.
   - ☐ b. the neighboring village.
   - ☐ c. advancing civilization.

10. The barricade had recently been
    - ☐ a. strengthened.
    - ☐ b. removed.
    - ☐ c. abandoned.

"By the way," said Dr. Ansell one evening when Morel was in Sheffield, "we've got a man in the fever hospital here who comes from Nottingham—Dawes. He doesn't seem to have many belongings in the world."

"Baxter Dawes!" Paul exclaimed.

"That's the man—has been a fine fellow, physically, I should think. Been in a bit of a mess lately—you know him?"

"He used to work at the place where I am."

"Did he? Do you know anything about him? He's just sulking, or he'd be a lot better than he is by now."

"I don't know anything of his home circumstances, except that he's separated from his wife and has been a bit down, I believe. But tell him about me, will you? Tell him I'll come and see him."

The next time Morel saw the doctor he said:

"And what about Dawes?"

"I said to him," answered the other, " 'Do you know a man from Nottingham named Morel?' and he looked at me as if he'd jump at my throat. So I said: 'I see you know the name; it's Paul Morel.' Then I told him about your saying you would go and see him. 'What does he want?' he said, as if you were a policeman."

"And did he say he would see me?" asked Paul.

"He wouldn't say anything—good, bad, or indifferent," replied the doctor.

"Why not?"

"That's what I want to know. There he lies and sulks, day in, day out—can't get a word of information out of him."

"Do you think I might go?" asked Paul.

"You might."

There was a feeling of connection between the rival men, more than ever since they had fought. In a way Morel felt guilty towards the other, and more or less responsible. And being in such a state of soul himself, he felt an almost painful nearness to Dawes, who was suffering and despairing, too. Besides, they had met in a naked extremity of hate, and it was a bond. At any rate, the elemental man in each had met.

He went down to the isolation hospital, with Dr. Ansell's card. The nurse, a healthy young Irishwoman, led him down the ward.

"A visitor to see you," she said.

Dawes looked swiftly with his dark, startled eyes beyond the nurse at Paul. His look was full of fear, mistrust, hate, and misery.

Recalling Facts

1. Dawes came from
   - ☐ a. Sheffield.
   - ☐ b. Nottingham.
   - ☐ c. St. Paul's.

2. Dawes was
   - ☐ a. separated from his wife.
   - ☐ b. recovering from a broken leg.
   - ☐ c. an extremely wealthy man.

3. Dawes was currently staying in
   - ☐ a. a fever hospital.
   - ☐ b. a friend's house.
   - ☐ c. an inn on the outskirts of town.

4. Morel and Dawes
   - ☐ a. were business partners.
   - ☐ b. had previously had a fight.
   - ☐ c. were old and close friends.

5. When Dawes saw Morel, his look was full of
   - ☐ a. surprise.
   - ☐ b. fear.
   - ☐ c. joy.

Understanding the Passage

6. Apparently Dawes was
   - ☐ a. having a streak of bad luck.
   - ☐ b. injured in a train wreck.
   - ☐ c. arrested by the police.

7. When Dawes heard Morel's name, he became
   - ☐ a. violent.
   - ☐ b. calm.
   - ☐ c. suspicious.

8. The doctor
   - ☐ a. knew what was troubling Dawes.
   - ☐ b. suggested that Morel stay away.
   - ☐ c. couldn't figure out what troubled Dawes.

9. The doctor believed Dawes should be
   - ☐ a. improving more quickly.
   - ☐ b. operated on as soon as possible.
   - ☐ c. protected from Morel.

10. Morel felt
    - ☐ a. bitter anger towards Dawes.
    - ☐ b. some sense of guilt about Dawes.
    - ☐ c. shock that Dawes was still alive.

"What is this all about?" cried Dorian, flinging himself down on the sofa. "I hope it is not about myself. I am tired of myself tonight. I should like to be somebody else."

"It is about yourself," answered Hallward, in his grave, deep voice, "and I must say it to you. I shall only keep you half an hour."

Dorian sighed. "Half an hour!" he murmured.

"It is not much to ask of you, Dorian, and it is entirely for your own sake that I am speaking. I think it right that you should know that the most dreadful things are being said against you in London."

"I don't wish to know anything about them. I love scandals about other people, but scandals about myself don't interest me. They have not got the charm of novelty."

"They must interest you, Dorian. Every gentleman is interested in his good name. You don't want people to talk of you as something vile and degraded. Of course you have your position, and your wealth, and all that kind of thing. But position and wealth are not everything. Mind you, I don't believe these rumors at all. At least, I can't believe them when I see you. Sin is a thing that writes itself across a man's face. It cannot be concealed. People talk sometimes of secret vices. There are no such things. If a wretched man has a vice, it shows itself in the lines of his mouth, the droop of his eyelids, the molding of his hands even. Somebody—I won't mention his name, but you know him—came to me last year to have a portrait done. I had never seen him before, and had never heard anything about him at the time, though I have heard a good deal since. He offered an extravagant price I refused him. There was something in the shape of his fingers that I hated. I know now that I was quite right in what I fancied about him. His life is dreadful. But you, Dorian, with your pure, bright, innocent face, and your marvelous untroubled youth—I can't believe anything against you. And yet I see you very seldom, and you never come down to the studio now, and when I am away from you, and I heard all these hideous things that people are whispering about you, I don't know what to say."

Recalling Facts

1. Hallward had heard
   - ☐ a. good things about Dorian.
   - ☐ b. nasty things about Dorian.
   - ☐ c. nothing about Dorian.

2. Dorian did not want to hear rumors about
   - ☐ a. his brother.
   - ☐ b. his friends.
   - ☐ c. himself.

3. Hallward believed that no man can
   - ☐ a. conceal his vices.
   - ☐ b. understand love.
   - ☐ c. be happy living alone.

4. Dorian had not recently been
   - ☐ a. to London.
   - ☐ b. to Hallward's studio.
   - ☐ c. home.

5. Hallward refused to paint a man's portrait because he did not like the
   - ☐ a. man's family.
   - ☐ b. shape of the man's fingers.
   - ☐ c. reputation of the man.

Understanding the Passage

6. Hallward's intention was to
   - ☐ a. help Dorian.
   - ☐ b. anger Dorian.
   - ☐ c. confuse Dorian.

7. Apparently, Dorian was
   - ☐ a. an old man.
   - ☐ b. a blind man.
   - ☐ c. a rich man.

8. Hallward did not want to
   - ☐ a. see Dorian.
   - ☐ b. believe the rumors he had heard.
   - ☐ c. leave Dorian alone even for a minute.

9. Hallward believed that Dorian had a
   - ☐ a. guilty look about him.
   - ☐ b. look of complete innocence.
   - ☐ c. dazed and confused look.

10. Dorian did not seem to care
   - ☐ a. how long Hallward stayed.
   - ☐ b. what other people thought of him.
   - ☐ c. both a and b.

34   *from* **Red Badge of Courage** *by Stephen Crane*

At nightfall the column broke into regimental pieces, and the fragments went into the fields to camp. Tents sprang up like strange plants. Camp fires, like red, peculiar blossoms, dotted the night. The youth kept from intercourse with his companions as much as circumstances would allow him. In the evening he wandered a few paces into the gloom. From this little distance the many fires, with the black forms of men passing to and fro before the crimson rays, made weird and satanic effects.

He lay down in the grass. The blades pressed tenderly against his cheek. The moon had been lighted and was hung in a treetop. The liquid stillness of the night enveloping him made him feel vast pity for himself. There was a caress in the soft winds; and the whole mood of the darkness, he thought, was one of sympathy for himself in his distress.

He wished that he was at home again making the endless rounds from the house to the barn, from the barn to the fields, from the fields to the barn, from the barn to the house. He remembered he had often cursed the brindle cow and her mates, and had sometimes flung milking stools. But, from his present point of view, there was a halo of happiness about each of their heads, and he would have sacrificed all the brass buttons on the continent to have been enabled to return to them. He told himself that he was not formed for a solider. And he mused seriously upon the radical differences between himself and those men who were dodging imp-like around the fires. As he mused thus he heard the rustle of grass. Upon turning his head, he discovered the loud soldier. He called out, "Oh, Wilson!"

The latter approached and looked down. "Why, hello, Henry; is it you? What you doing here?"

"Oh, thinking," said the youth.

The other sat down and carefully lighted his pipe. "You're getting blue, my boy. You're looking thundering peeked. What the dickens is wrong with you?"

"Oh, nothing," said the youth.

The loud soldier launched then into the subject of the anticipated fight. "Oh, we've got 'em now!" As he spoke his boyish face was wreathed in a gleeful smile, and his voice had an exultant ring. "We've got 'em now. By the eternal thunders, we'll lick 'em good!"

---

*Reading Time*_____   *Comprehension Score*_____   *Words per Minute*_____   81

Recalling Facts

1. The men in the regiment slept
   - ☐ a. in barracks.
   - ☐ b. deep in the woods.
   - ☐ c. in tents.

2. The youth tried
   - ☐ a. not to talk to the other men.
   - ☐ b. to warm himself by a campfire.
   - ☐ c. to run away.

3. The night was
   - ☐ a. cloudy.
   - ☐ b. rainy.
   - ☐ c. moonlit.

4. At one time the youth had cursed
   - ☐ a. his parents.
   - ☐ b. his cows.
   - ☐ c. brass buttons.

5. The youth's name was
   - ☐ a. Wilson.
   - ☐ b. Henry.
   - ☐ c. not mentioned.

Understanding the Passage

6. The youth felt that he
   - ☐ a. couldn't wait for the next battle.
   - ☐ b. was fighting on the wrong side.
   - ☐ c. was in a very sad state.

7. The youth wanted nothing more than to
   - ☐ a. return to his farm.
   - ☐ b. talk to his friends.
   - ☐ c. fall asleep on the grass.

8. The youth was convinced that he was not cut out for
   - ☐ a. a military career.
   - ☐ b. farming.
   - ☐ c. sleeping in a tent.

9. When the loud soldier arrived, the youth
   - ☐ a. talked without stopping.
   - ☐ b. gave short answers.
   - ☐ c. ignored him.

10. The loud soldier boasted about the upcoming
    - ☐ a. battle.
    - ☐ b. peace treaty.
    - ☐ c. promotion.

All at once I heard a heavy step approaching behind the great door. I saw through the chinks the gleam of a coming light. There was the sound of rattling chains and the clanking of massive bolts drawn back. A key was turned with the loud grating noise of long disuse. Then the great door swung back.

Within, stood a tall old man, clean shaven save for a long white moustache. He was clad in black from head to foot, without a single speck of color about him anywhere. He held in his hand an antique silver lamp, in which the flame burned without chimney or globe of any kind, throwing long quivering shadows as it flickered in the draft of the open door. The old man motioned me in with his right hand with a courtly gesture, saying in excellent English, but with a strange intonation:

"Welcome to my house! Enter freely and of your own will!" He made no motion of stepping to meet me, but stood like a statue. It was as though his gesture of welcome had fixed him into stone. The instant, however, that I had stepped over the threshold, he moved impulsively forward, and holding out his hand grasped mine with a strength which made me wince. The effect was not lessened by the fact that it seemed as cold as ice—more like the hand of a dead than a living man. Again he said:

"Welcome to my house. Come freely. Go safely; and leave something of the happiness you bring!" The strength of the handshake was so much akin to that which I had noticed in the driver, whose face I had not seen, that for a moment I doubted if it were not the same person to whom I was speaking. To make sure, I said:

"Count Dracula?" He bowed in a courtly way as he replied:

"I am Dracula. I bid you welcome, Mr. Harker, to my house. Come in. The night air is chill, and you must need to eat and rest." As he was speaking, he put the lamp on a bracket on the wall, and stepping out, took my luggage. He had carried it in before I could forestall him. I protested but he insisted:

"Nay, sir, you are my guest. It is late, and my people are not available. Let me see to your comfort myself."

Recalling Facts

1. The narrator heard
   - ☐ a. a heavy step.
   - ☐ b. rattling chains.
   - ☐ c. both a and b.

2. Within the great door stood a
   - ☐ a. tall old man.
   - ☐ b. short fat man.
   - ☐ c. slender young woman.

3. The person within the great door carried a
   - ☐ a. silver lamp.
   - ☐ b. globe of light.
   - ☐ c. lighted candle.

4. The narrator (the person telling this story) was greeted with
   - ☐ a. a tip of the hat.
   - ☐ b. a strong, cold handshake.
   - ☐ c. the sound of singing birds.

5. The visitor's name was
   - ☐ a. Dracula.
   - ☐ b. Harker.
   - ☐ c. not mentioned.

Understanding the Passage

6. The house in this passage can best be described as
   - ☐ a. warm and friendly.
   - ☐ b. small and cozy.
   - ☐ c. large and frightening.

7. Dracula appeared to be
   - ☐ a. polite.
   - ☐ b. angry.
   - ☐ c. nervous.

8. The greeting "Enter freely and of your own will" suggests
   - ☐ a. a long visit.
   - ☐ b. some risk.
   - ☐ c. a pleasant welcome.

9. Apparently, the driver also had a
   - ☐ a. silver lamp.
   - ☐ b. courtly manner.
   - ☐ c. strong handshake.

10. The narrator wanted to
    - ☐ a. carry his own luggage.
    - ☐ b. leave the house immediately.
    - ☐ c. go straight to his room.

My new car, a thirty-horsepower Robur, had only been delivered that day. I asked Perkins, my chauffeur, how it had gone. He said that he thought it was excellent.

"I'll try it myself," said I, and I climbed into the driver's seat.

"The gears are not the same," said he. "Perhaps, sir, I had better drive."

"No; I should like to try it," said I.

And so we started on the five-mile drive for home.

My old car had the gears as they always used to be in notches on a bar. In this car you passed the gear lever through a gate to get on the higher ones. It was not difficult to master, and soon I thought that I understood it. It was foolish, no doubt, to begin to learn a new system in the dark. But one often does foolish things, and one has not always to pay the full price for them. I got along very well until I came to Claystall Hill. It is one of the worst hills in England, a mile and a half long, with three fairly sharp curves. My park gates stand at the very foot of it upon the main London road.

We were just over the brow of this hill, where the grade is steepest, when the trouble began. I had been on the top speed, and wanted to get it on the free; but it stuck between gears, and I had to get it back on the top again. By this time it was going at a great rate, so I clapped on both brakes. One after the other they gave way. I didn't mind so much when I felt my footbrake snap, but when I put all my weight on my side brake, and the lever clanged to its full limit without a catch, it brought a cold sweat out of me. By this time we were fairly tearing down the slope. The lights were brilliant, and I brought it round the first curve all right. Then we did the second one, though it was a close shave for the ditch. There was a mile of straight then with the third curve beneath it, and after that the gate of the park. If I could shoot into that harbor all would be well, for the slope up to the house would bring it to a stand.

Recalling Facts

1. Perkins thought the Robur was
   - ☐ a. a troublesome car.
   - ☐ b. a fair car.
   - ☐ c. an excellent car.

2. The narrator took his test drive in
   - ☐ a. brilliant sunlight.
   - ☐ b. the dark.
   - ☐ c. the fog.

3. Claystall Hill was one of the worst hills in
   - ☐ a. England.
   - ☐ b. the United States.
   - ☐ c. Ireland.

4. The narrator had trouble with the car's
   - ☐ a. motor.
   - ☐ b. gears.
   - ☐ c. steering wheel.

5. Claystall Hill had
   - ☐ a. three sharp curves.
   - ☐ b. six sharp curves.
   - ☐ c. no sharp curves.

Understanding the Passage

6. The narrator had
   - ☐ a. never driven a Robur before.
   - ☐ b. driven a Robur for years.
   - ☐ c. never allowed Perkins to drive his car.

7. In taking the car out for a drive when he did, the narrator
   - ☐ a. was taking a chance.
   - ☐ b. offended Perkins.
   - ☐ c. expected to run into trouble.

8. The narrator was unfamiliar with the Robur's
   - ☐ a. gear system.
   - ☐ b. steering bar.
   - ☐ c. high speed.

9. The new car had poor
   - ☐ a. steering.
   - ☐ b. brakes.
   - ☐ c. headlights.

10. As the car plunged down the hill, the narrator
    - ☐ a. was terribly frightened.
    - ☐ b. planned to jump out the door.
    - ☐ c. stayed fairly calm.

I regret to say that Nat sometimes told lies. They were not very black ones, seldom getting deeper than gray, and often the mildest of white fibs. But that did not matter, a lie is a lie, and though we all tell many polite untruths in this queer world of ours, it is not right, and everybody knows it.

"You cannot be too careful; watch your tongue, and eyes and hands, for it is easy to tell, and look, and act untruth," said Mr. Bhaer, in one of the talks he had with Nat.

"I know it, and I don't mean to, but it's so much easier to get along if you ain't very fussy about being exactly true. I used to tell 'em because I was afraid of father and Nicolo. Now I do sometimes because the boys laugh at me. I know it's bad, but I forget," and Nat looked much depressed by his sins.

"When I was a little lad I used to tell lies! Ach! what fibs they were, and my old grandmother cured me of it—how, do you think? My parents had talked, and cried, and punished, but still did I forget as you. Then said the dear old grandmother, 'I shall help you to remember, and put a check on this unruly part,' with that she drew out my tongue and snipped the end with her scissors till the blood ran. That was terrible, you may believe, but it did me much good, because it was sore for days, and every word I said came so slowly that I had time to think."

"I never had any grandmothers. But if you think it will cure me, I'll let you snip my tongue," said Nat, heroically, for he dreaded pain, yet did wish to stop fibbing.

Mr. Bhaer smiled, but shook his head.

"I have a better way than that. I tried it once before and it worked well. See now, when you tell a lie I will not punish you, but you shall punish me."

"How?" asked Nat, startled at the idea.

"You shall whip me in the good old-fashioned way. I seldom do it myself, but it may make you remember better to give me pain than to feel it yourself."

"Strike you? Oh, I couldn't!" cried Nat.

"Then mind that tripping tongue of thine. I have no wish to be hurt."

Recalling Facts

1. The lies Nat told were often
   □ a. unbelievable.
   □ b. cruel and hurtful.
   □ c. white fibs.

2. Mr. Bhaer told Nat that
   telling lies was
   □ a. dangerously easy to do.
   □ b. nothing to worry about.
   □ c. one of the things
       boys did.

3. Nat's lying
   □ a. did not bother him.
   □ b. depressed him.
   □ c. made Nicolo laugh.

4. Mr. Bhaer's grandmother
   snipped the end of his
   □ a. finger.
   □ b. nose.
   □ c. tongue.

5. If Nat did not stop lying,
   Mr. Bhaer promised punish-
   ment for
   □ a. Nat.
   □ b. all the boys.
   □ c. himself.

Understanding the Passage

6. The narrator felt that lies
   □ a. were all equally bad.
   □ b. ranged from good
       to bad.
   □ c. did not hurt anyone.

7. Mr. Bhaer wanted to
   □ a. hurt Nat.
   □ b. ignore Nat.
   □ c. cure Nat.

8. Nat lied to some people
   because he
   □ a. didn't want to be
       laughed at.
   □ b. was afraid of them.
   □ c. both a and b.

9. The grandmother's cure
   for lying was
   □ a. not very attractive.
   □ b. cruel, but effective.
   □ c. used by many adults.

10. Mr. Bhaer believed he could
    □ a. help Nat.
    □ b. do nothing for Nat.
    □ c. never forgive Nat.

From the mountain path came the sound of a person whistling with good humor and undaunted courage. The whistler was Rudy. He was going to his friend Vesinand.

"You must help me!" he called as he approached Vesinand. "We shall take Ragli with us. I must capture the young eagle up yonder under the shelving rock!"

"Had you not better try first to take down the moon? That would be about as hopeful an undertaking," said Vesinand. "You are in great spirits, I see."

"Yes, for I am thinking of my wedding. But now, to speak seriously, let me tell you what I am planning."

And Vesinand and Ragli soon found out what Rudy wished.

"You are a daring fellow," they said, "but you won't succeed. You will break your neck."

"One does not fall if one has no fear!" said Rudy.

About midnight they set out with alpenstocks, ladders, and ropes. The road lay through copsewood and brushwood, over rolling stones—upward, always upward, upward in the dark and gloomy night. The waters roared below, the waters murmured above, humid clouds swept heavily along. The hunters reached at length the precipitous ridge of rock. It became even darker here, for the walls of rock almost met, and light penetrated only a little way down from the open space above. Close by, under them, was a deep abyss, with its hoarse-sounding, raging water.

They sat all three quite still. They had to await the dawn of day, when the parent eagle should fly out. Only then could they shoot it if they had any hope to capture the young one. Rudy sat as still as if he had been a portion of the rock on which he sat. He held his gun ready to fire. His eyes were steadily fixed on the highest part of the cleft, under a projecting rock on which the eagle's nest was concealed. The three hunters had long to wait.

At length, high above them was heard a crashing, whirring noise. The air was darkened by a large object soaring in it. Two guns were ready to aim at the enormous eagle the moment it flew from its nest. A shot was fired. For an instant the outspread wings fluttered. Then the bird began to sink slowly and it seemed as if with its size and the stretch of its wings it would fill the whole chasm.

Recalling Facts

1. Vesinand was Rudy's
   - ☐ a. father-in-law.
   - ☐ b. friend.
   - ☐ c. teacher.

2. Rudy wanted to
   - ☐ a. capture a young eagle.
   - ☐ b. collect feathers.
   - ☐ c. take down the moon.

3. The equipment the boys took included
   - ☐ a. flashlights.
   - ☐ b. axes.
   - ☐ c. ropes.

4. Rudy, Vesinand, and Ragli set off on their adventure
   - ☐ a. at sunrise.
   - ☐ b. just after noon.
   - ☐ c. about midnight.

5. The boys sat waiting
   - ☐ a. in the desert.
   - ☐ b. by the broad river.
   - ☐ c. on a high rock.

Understanding the Passage

6. When he met Vesinand, Rudy was
   - ☐ a. sad and depressed.
   - ☐ b. brimming with confidence.
   - ☐ c. extremely anxious.

7. Rudy could not achieve his goal
   - ☐ a. easily.
   - ☐ b. by himself.
   - ☐ c. both a and b.

8. Vesinand thought Rudy was
   - ☐ a. taking a huge chance.
   - ☐ b. an excellent hunter.
   - ☐ c. an experienced rock climber.

9. The boys prepared themselves to do a lot of
   - ☐ a. sleeping.
   - ☐ b. climbing.
   - ☐ c. swimming.

10. During the long wait, Rudy
    - ☐ a. fell asleep.
    - ☐ b. showed great patience.
    - ☐ c. became more and more irritable.

I opened the door and could see nobody. I dried my tears and looked all round the room—it was empty. I ran upstairs again to Uncle George's garret bedroom—he was not there. His cheap hairbrush and old cast-off razor case that had belonged to my grandfather were not on the dressing table. Had he got some other bedroom? I went out on the landing, and called softly, with terror and sinking at my heart—

"Uncle George!"

Nobody answered; but my aunt came hastily up the garret stairs.

"Hush!" she said. "You must never say that name out here again!"

She stopped suddenly and looked as if her own words had frightened her.

"Is Uncle George dead?" I asked.

My aunt turned red and pale, and stammered.

I did not wait to hear what she said. I brushed past her, down the stairs. My heart was bursting—my flesh felt cold. I ran breathlessly and recklessly into the room where my father and mother had received me. They were both sitting there still. I ran up to them, wringing my hands, and crying out in a passion of tears,

"Is Uncle George dead?"

My mother gave a scream that terrified me into silence. My father looked at her for a moment, rang the bell that summoned the maid, then seized me by the arm and dragged me out of the room.

He took me down into the study, seated himself in his accustomed chair, and put me before him between his knees. His lips were awfully white, and I felt his two hands as they grasped my shoulders, shaking violently.

"You are never to mention the name of Uncle George again," he said, in a quick, angry, trembling whisper. "Never to me, never to your mother, never to your aunt, never to anybody in this world! Never—never—never!"

The repetition of the word terrified me even more than the anger with which he spoke. He saw that I was frightened and softened his manner a little before he went on."

"You will never see Uncle George again," he said. "Your mother and I love you dearly; but if you forget what I have told you, you will be sent away from home. Never speak that name again—mind, never! Now kiss me, and go away."

How his lips trembled—and oh, how cold they felt on mine!

Recalling Facts

1. The narrator looked for Uncle George in
   - ☐ a. his office.
   - ☐ b. the kitchen.
   - ☐ c. his bedroom.

2. The narrator was first told not to use Uncle George's name by his
   - ☐ a. aunt.
   - ☐ b. father.
   - ☐ c. sister.

3. The narrator was dragged out of the room by his
   - ☐ a. uncle.
   - ☐ b. brother.
   - ☐ c. father.

4. The narrator feared that Uncle George was
   - ☐ a. sick.
   - ☐ b. missing.
   - ☐ c. dead.

5. The narrator was surprised by his father's
   - ☐ a. uncontrolled sobbing.
   - ☐ b. cold lips.
   - ☐ c. both a and b.

Understanding the Passage

6. At the beginning of this passage, the narrator had been
   - ☐ a. happy.
   - ☐ b. laughing.
   - ☐ c. crying.

7. The missing hairbrush and razor case were clues that
   - ☐ a. someone had broken into the bedroom.
   - ☐ b. Uncle George was gone.
   - ☐ c. the police had already collected evidence.

8. Uncle George appeared to be much loved by the
   - ☐ a. narrator.
   - ☐ b. narrator's aunt.
   - ☐ c. narrator's mother.

9. The father wanted to make sure that the narrator
   - ☐ a. remembered Uncle George.
   - ☐ b. stopped crying.
   - ☐ c. understood him.

10. The narrator's reaction to Uncle George's disappearance was one of
    - ☐ a. joy.
    - ☐ b. relief.
    - ☐ c. distress.

"Now, boys," said Lane, "keep your eyes open. Walk around the house and watch the road well. All of you know McRoy, or the 'Frio Kid,' as they call him now. If you see him, open fire without asking any questions. I'm not afraid of his coming, but Rosita is. She's been afraid he'd come in on us every Christmas since we were married."

The evening went along nicely. The guests praised Rosita's fine supper. Afterward the men scattered in groups about the rooms.

The Christmas tree, of course, delighted the youngsters. But most of all they were pleased when Santa Claus himself in flowing white beard and furs appeared and began to give out the toys.

"It's my papa," said Billy Sampson, aged six. "I've seen him wear 'em before."

Berkly, a sheepman, an old friend of Lane, stopped Rosita as she was passing by him on the gallery, where he was sitting smoking.

"Well, Mrs. Lane," said he, "I suppose by this Christmas you've gotten over being afraid of that fellow McRoy, haven't you? Madison and I have talked about it, you know."

"Very nearly," said Rosita, smiling, "but I am still nervous sometimes. I shall never forget the awful time when he came so near to killing us."

"He's the most cold-hearted villain in the world," said Berkly. "The citizens all along the border ought to turn out and hunt him down like a wolf."

"He has committed awful crimes," said Rosita, "but—I—don't—know. I think there is a spot of good somewhere in everybody. He was not always bad—that I know."

Rosita turned into the hallway between the rooms. Santa Claus, in muffling whiskers and furs, was just coming through.

"I heard what you said through the window, Mrs. Lane," he said. "I was just going down in my pocket for a Christmas present for your husband. But I've left one for you, instead. It's in the room to your right."

"Oh, thank you, kind Santa Claus," said Rosita, brightly.

She went into the room, while Santa Claus stepped into the cooler air of the yard.

She found no one in the room but Madison.

"Where is my present that Santa said he left for me?" she asked.

"Haven't seen anything in the way of a present," said her husband, laughing, "unless he could have meant me."

Recalling Facts

1. Lane told the men to keep a close watch for
   - ☐ a. Rosita.
   - ☐ b. Billy Sampson.
   - ☐ c. McRoy.

2. The guests praised Rosita for her fine
   - ☐ a. supper.
   - ☐ b. presents.
   - ☐ c. linen.

3. Billy Sampson thought Santa Claus was
   - ☐ a. his father.
   - ☐ b. the "Frio Kid."
   - ☐ c. Mr. Lane.

4. Santa Claus told Rosita that her Christmas present was
   - ☐ a. under the tree.
   - ☐ b. near the fireplace.
   - ☐ c. in the room to her right.

5. Madison told Rosita that
   - ☐ a. Santa Claus had left.
   - ☐ b. he knew of no present.
   - ☐ c. someone had seen the "Frio Kid."

Understanding the Passage

6. The "Frio Kid" was
   - ☐ a. a dinner guest.
   - ☐ b. a sheepman.
   - ☐ c. an outlaw.

7. Rosita was an excellent
   - ☐ a. gunfighter.
   - ☐ b. cook.
   - ☐ c. storyteller.

8. Rosita believed that
   - ☐ a. no one was completely bad.
   - ☐ b. her fears were unreasonable.
   - ☐ c. the "Frio Kid" was nearby.

9. Santa Claus did not give
   - ☐ a. any gifts to the children.
   - ☐ b. Rosita's husband a present.
   - ☐ c. both a and b.

10. Rosita had been
    - ☐ a. an old childhood friend of the "Frio Kid."
    - ☐ b. almost killed by the "Frio Kid."
    - ☐ c. present when the "Frio Kid" robbed several banks.

Koolau was alone in the gorge. He watched the last of his people drag their crippled bodies over the brow of the height and disappear. Then he turned and went down to the thicket where the maid had been killed. The shell-fire still continued, but he remained; for far below he could see the soldiers climbing up. A shell burst twenty feet away. Flattening himself into the earth, he heard the rush of the fragments above his body. A shower of hau blossoms rained upon him. He lifted his head to peer down the trail, and sighed. He was very much afraid. Bullets from rifles would not have worried him, but this shellfire was abominable. Each time a shell shrieked by he shivered and crouched; but each time he lifted his head again to watch the trail.

At last the shells ceased. This, he reasoned, was because the soldiers were drawing near. They crept along the trail in single file, and he tried to count them until he lost track. At any rate, there were a hundred or so of them—all come after Koolau the leper. He felt a fleeting prod of pride. With war guns and rifles, police and soldiers, they came for him, and he was only one man, a crippled wreck of a man at that. They offered a thousand dollars for him, dead or alive. In all his life he had never possessed that much money. The thought was a bitter one. Kapahei had been right. He, Koolau, had done no wrong. Because the whites wanted labor with which to work the stolen land, they had brought in the Chinese coolies, and with them had come the sickness. And now, because he had caught the sickness, he was worth a thousand dollars—but not to himself. It was his worthless carcass, rotten with disease or dead from a bursting shell, that was worth all that money.

When the soldiers reached the knife-edged passage, he was prompted to warn them. But his gaze fell upon the body of the murdered maid, and he kept silent. When six had ventured on the knife edge, he opened fire. Nor did he cease when the knife edge was bare. He emptied his magazine, reloaded, and emptied it again. He kept on shooting. All his wrongs were blazing in his brain, and he was in a fury of vengeance.

Recalling Facts

1. Koolau's people disappeared
   - ☐ a. into the thicket.
   - ☐ b. over the side of the knife-edged passage.
   - ☐ c. over the brow of the height.

2. Koolau feared
   - ☐ a. bullets.
   - ☐ b. shellfire.
   - ☐ c. daggers.

3. The reward for capturing Koolau was
   - ☐ a. one hundred dollars.
   - ☐ b. one thousand dollars.
   - ☐ c. ten thousand dollars.

4. When Chinese coolies came to the area, they brought with them
   - ☐ a. new forms of plant life.
   - ☐ b. hau blossoms.
   - ☐ c. sickness.

5. The maid had been
   - ☐ a. murdered.
   - ☐ b. a spy.
   - ☐ c. handsomely rewarded.

Understanding the Passage

6. Koolau could best be described as
   - ☐ a. bitter.
   - ☐ b. silly.
   - ☐ c. generous.

7. Koolau was crippled from
   - ☐ a. a hunting accident.
   - ☐ b. disease.
   - ☐ c. a soldier's bullet.

8. The soldiers were prepared to
   - ☐ a. let Koolau escape.
   - ☐ b. compromise with Koolau.
   - ☐ c. kill Koolau.

9. Koolau and his people were
   - ☐ a. coolies.
   - ☐ b. lepers.
   - ☐ c. gamblers.

10. Koolau was ready to
    - ☐ a. surrender.
    - ☐ b. fight.
    - ☐ c. sleep.

42 *from* **The Posthumous Papers of the Pickwick Club** *by Charles Dickens*

"For nearly a year I saw my wife's face grow paler; for nearly a year I saw the tears steal down the mournful cheeks, and never knew the cause. I found it out at last, though. They could not keep it from me long. She had never liked me; I had never thought she did: she despised my wealth, and hated the splendor in which she lived—I had not expected that. She loved another. This I had never thought of. Strange feelings came over me, and thoughts, forced upon me by some secret power, whirled round and round my brain. I did not hate her, though I hated the boy she still wept for. I pitied—yes, I pitied—the wretched life to which her cold and selfish relations had doomed her. I knew that she could not live long, but the thought that before her death she might give birth to some ill-fated being, destined to hand down madness to its offspring, determined me. I resolved to kill her.

"For many weeks I thought of poison, and then of drowning, and then of fire. A fine sight the grand house in flames, and the madman's wife smouldering away to cinders. I thought often of this, but I gave it up at last. Oh! the pleasure of stropping the razor day after day, feeling the sharp edge, and thinking of the gash one stroke of its thin bright edge would make!

"At last the old spirits who had been with me so often before whispered in my ear that the time was come, and thrust the open razor into my hand. I grasped it firmly, rose softly from the bed, and leaned over my sleeping wife. Her face was buried in her hands. I withdrew them softly, and they fell listlessly on her bosom. She had been weeping; for the traces of the tears were still wet upon her cheek. Her face was calm; and even as I looked upon it, a tranquil smile lighted up her pale features. I laid my hand softly on her shoulder. She started—it was only a passing dream. I leant forward again. She screamed, and woke.

"One motion of my hand, and she would never again have uttered cry or sound. But I was startled, and drew back. Her eyes were fixed on mine. I know not how it was, but they frightened me."

Recalling Facts

1. The speaker's wife
   - ☐ a. was in love with someone else.
   - ☐ b. loved no one but her boy.
   - ☐ c. loved her husband more than her children.

2. The speaker thought of
   - ☐ a. poisoning his wife.
   - ☐ b. drowning his wife.
   - ☐ c. both a and b.

3. The speaker finally decided to kill his wife with
   - ☐ a. fire.
   - ☐ b. a razor.
   - ☐ c. a gun.

4. The speaker came into his wife's bedroom while she was
   - ☐ a. singing.
   - ☐ b. weeping.
   - ☐ c. sleeping.

5. When the wife fixed her eyes on the speaker, he became
   - ☐ a. filled with rage.
   - ☐ b. filled with love.
   - ☐ c. frightened.

Understanding the Passage

6. The speaker's wife was
   - ☐ a. unhappily married.
   - ☐ b. happy to be rich.
   - ☐ c. much older than her husband.

7. The speaker did not want his wife to
   - ☐ a. give birth to a child.
   - ☐ b. die of unhappiness.
   - ☐ c. keep laughing at him.

8. The speaker's wife
   - ☐ a. kept secrets from him.
   - ☐ b. pitied him.
   - ☐ c. begged him for forgiveness.

9. This passage is about human
   - ☐ a. greed.
   - ☐ b. madness.
   - ☐ c. kindness.

10. The speaker can best be described as
   - ☐ a. caring and loving.
   - ☐ b. dangerous and cunning.
   - ☐ c. calm and thoughtful.

"I'm unhappy, Miss Ingate," said Audrey. "Now if I wanted to make the best marmalade you ever tasted in your born days, first of all there would be a fearful row about the oranges. Secondly father would tell mother she must tell me exactly what I was to do. He would also tell cook. Thirdly and lastly, dear friends, he would come into the kitchen himself. It wouldn't be my marmalade at all. I should only be a marmalade-making machine. They never let me have any responsibility—not even when mother's operation was on—and I am never truly free. The kitchen maid has far more responsibility than I have, and she has an evening off and an afternoon off. She can write a letter without everybody asking her who she's writing to. She's only seventeen, but she has money and she buys her own clothes. She's a very naughty, wicked girl, and I wish I was in her place. She scorns me, naturally—who wouldn't?"

Miss Ingate said nothing. She merely sat with her hands in the lap of her pale blue dress, faintly and sadly smiling. Audrey burst out, "Miss Ingate, what can I do? I must do something—but what?"

Miss Ingate shook her head, and put her lips tightly together, while smoothing the sides of her grey coat. "I don't know," she said.

"Then *I'll* tell you what I can do!" answered Audrey firmly, wriggling nearer to her along the floor. "And what I definitely shall do. Will you promise to keep it a secret?"

"Yes," Miss Ingate nodded. She smiled, showing her teeth. Her broad polished forehead shone with kindly eagerness.

"Will you swear?"

Miss Ingate hesitated. Then she nodded again.

"Then put your hand on my head and say, 'I swear.' "

Miss Ingate obeyed.

"I shall leave this house," said Audrey in a low voice.

"You won't, Audrey!"

"I'll eat my hand off if I've not left this house by tomorrow."

"Tomorrow!" Miss Ingate practically screamed. "Now, Audrey, do reflect a minute. Think what you are!"

Audrey bounded to her feet.

"That's what father is always saying," she exploded angrily. "He is always telling me to examine myself. The fact is I know too much about myself. I know exactly the kind of girl it is who's going to leave this house. Exactly!"

"Audrey, you frighten me. Where are you going to?"

"London."

Recalling Facts

1. Audrey was
   - ☐ a. unhappy.
   - ☐ b. excited.
   - ☐ c. disappointed.

2. The kitchen maid was only
   - ☐ a. fifteen.
   - ☐ b. seventeen.
   - ☐ c. nineteen.

3. Miss Ingate promised to
   - ☐ a. lend Audrey money.
   - ☐ b. speak to the kitchen maid.
   - ☐ c. keep Audrey's secret.

4. Audrey planned to leave
   - ☐ a. in a month.
   - ☐ b. in a week.
   - ☐ c. the next day.

5. Audrey's father often told Audrey to
   - ☐ a. stop complaining.
   - ☐ b. make marmalade.
   - ☐ c. examine herself.

Understanding the Passage

6. Audrey planned to
   - ☐ a. confront her father.
   - ☐ b. meet with the kitchen maid.
   - ☐ c. run away from home.

7. Audrey felt she needed
   - ☐ a. a more loving mother.
   - ☐ b. more freedom.
   - ☐ c. help making marmalade.

8. Audrey envied
   - ☐ a. her father.
   - ☐ b. Miss Ingate.
   - ☐ c. the kitchen maid.

9. When she heard Audrey's plan, Miss Ingate was
   - ☐ a. delighted.
   - ☐ b. uninterested.
   - ☐ c. distressed.

10. Audrey was
   - ☐ a. determined to leave.
   - ☐ b. comforted by Miss Ingate.
   - ☐ c. furious at the kitchen maid.

44 *from* **Buried Alive** *by Feodor Dostoyevski*

"Sirotkin, how can you be a murderer?"

"It is quite true, Alexander Petrovitch. My life was so very hard that I was driven to do it."

"But how do the other recruits bear it? Nobody expects a soldier's life to be very easy, but they get used to its hardships, and by and by become good soldiers. I fear, my friend, that your mother spoiled you, and stuffed you with milk and gingerbread till you were eighteen years old."

"Yes, sir, my mother did love me dearly. I have heard since that after I left her she took to her bed and never left it again. . . . Well, my life was terribly hard. My colonel took a dislike to me—I do not know why—and I was always being punished. And yet I tried to do my duty. I did, indeed; I was always good, never touched brandy, and never stole anything. But they seemed all to be such a hardhearted set, nobody had any pity for me, and I had no place where I could hide myself and have a good cry. Sometimes I would creep into a corner, and cry a little there. One night I was on guard. It was in autumn, the wind whistled in the trees, and the night was so dark that I could see nothing at all. I was walking up and down all by myself, and feeling so wretched. I cannot tell you how wretched I was. I took my gun from my shoulder, unscrewed the bayonet, and laid it on the ground. Then I pulled off my right boot, put the muzzle to my breast, leaned heavily on it, pressing down the trigger at the same time with my big toe. It misfired! I examined the gun carefully, cleaned it, loaded it afresh, and again put it to my breast. The powder flashed in the pan, but the gun misfired again. Well, I put on my boot, shouldered my gun, screwed on the bayonet, and again marched up and down. And then I made up my mind to do something desperate only to have done with that wretched life. Half an hour later up comes the colonel at the head of the patrol. What does he do but swear at me for not carrying my gun properly. So I took it in both hands, and stuck the bayonet right into him.

Recalling Facts

1. Alexander thought that Sirotkin was
   - ☐ a. a good soldier.
   - ☐ b. spoiled by his mother.
   - ☐ c. a cold-blooded killer.

2. The officer Sirotkin killed was a
   - ☐ a. major.
   - ☐ b. colonel.
   - ☐ c. captain.

3. Sirotkin's rifle misfired
   - ☐ a. once.
   - ☐ b. twice.
   - ☐ c. three times.

4. During this night Sirotkin was supposed to be
   - ☐ a. on guard.
   - ☐ b. in his foxhole.
   - ☐ c. back in the barracks.

5. Sirotkin killed the officer with
   - ☐ a. a bullet.
   - ☐ b. his bayonet.
   - ☐ c. a rock.

Understanding the Passage

6. Most young recruits
   - ☐ a. found military life difficult.
   - ☐ b. turned out to be good soldiers.
   - ☐ c. both a and b.

7. After Sirotkin left home, his mother
   - ☐ a. regained her health.
   - ☐ b. became ill.
   - ☐ c. died suddenly.

8. Sirotkin can best be described as
   - ☐ a. competent.
   - ☐ b. well liked.
   - ☐ c. very sensitive.

9. Sirotkin failed in his effort to
   - ☐ a. become a good officer.
   - ☐ b. commit suicide.
   - ☐ c. forgive his mother.

10. When Sirotkin killed the officer, he was
    - ☐ a. indifferent.
    - ☐ b. desperate.
    - ☐ c. jubilant.

The Swinton barbecue was over. The fiddles were silent, the steer was eaten, the barrel emptied, or largely so, and the candles extinguished. Round the house and sunken fire all movement of guests was quiet. The families were long departed homeward, and after their hospitable turbulence, the Swintons slept.

Mr. and Mrs. Westfall drove through the night, and as they neared their cabin there came from among the bundled wraps a still, small voice.

"Jim," said his wife, "I said Alfred would catch cold."

"Bosh! Lizzie, don't you fret. He's a little more than a yearlin', and of course he'll snuffle." And James kissed his wife.

"Well, how you can speak of Alfred that way, calling him a yearling, as if he was a calf, and he just as much your child as mine, I don't see, James Westfall!"

"Why, what under the sun do you mean?"

"There he goes again! Do hurry up home, Jim. He's got a real strange cough."

So they hurried home. Soon the nine miles were finished, and good James was unhitching the horses by his stable lantern, while his wife in the house hastened to commit their offspring to bed. The traces had dropped, and each horse marched forward for further unbuckling, when James heard himself called. Indeed, there was that in his wife's voice which made him jerk out his pistol as he ran. But it was no bear or intruder—only two strange children on the bed. His wife was glaring down at them. He sighed with relief and laid down the pistol.

"Put that on again, James Westfall. You'll need it. Look here!"

"Well, they won't bite. Whose are they? Where've you put ours?"

"Where have I—" Utterance forsook this mother for a moment. "And you ask me!" she continued. "Ask Lin McLean. Ask him that sets bulls on folks and steals slippers, what he's done with our innocent lambs, mixing them up with other people's coughing, unhealthy brats. That's Charlie Taylor in Alfred's clothes, and I know Alfred didn't cough like that, and I said to you it was strange; and the other one that's been put in Christopher's new quilts is not even a bub—bub—boy!"

As this crime against society loomed clear to James Westfall's mind, he sat down on the nearest piece of furniture, and heedless of his wife's tears and his exchanged children, broke into wild laughter.

Recalling Facts

1. Mr. and Mrs. Westfall lived in a
   - ☐ a. tent.
   - ☐ b. cabin.
   - ☐ c. hut.

2. Jim called Alfred a
   - ☐ a. yearling.
   - ☐ b. calf.
   - ☐ c. baby.

3. To get home from the barbecue, the Westfalls had to travel
   - ☐ a. two miles.
   - ☐ b. four miles.
   - ☐ c. nine miles.

4. James came running with his pistol drawn when he heard
   - ☐ a. his wife's voice.
   - ☐ b. the growl of a bear.
   - ☐ c. the sounds of children crying.

5. James's reaction to the news of the exchanged children was to
   - ☐ a. strap on his gun.
   - ☐ b. laugh.
   - ☐ c. cry.

Understanding the Passage

6. On the way home, the child's coughing
   - ☐ a. didn't seem to bother Jim.
   - ☐ b. proved that the child wasn't Alfred.
   - ☐ c. frightened his parents.

7. The children must have been
   - ☐ a. very hungry.
   - ☐ b. upset by the long ride.
   - ☐ c. bundled up from head to toe.

8. As Lizzie started to put the two children to bed, she
   - ☐ a. asked them to say their prayers.
   - ☐ b. got them some warm milk.
   - ☐ c. discovered something shocking.

9. Lizzie believed that the person responsible for the prank was
   - ☐ a. Charlie Taylor.
   - ☐ b. Lin McLean.
   - ☐ c. Christopher.

10. The true children of Mr. and Mrs. Westfall were
   - ☐ a. both girls.
   - ☐ b. a boy and a girl.
   - ☐ c. both boys.

"Max, you silly devil, you'll break your neck if you go careering down the slide that way. Drop it, and come to the Club House with me and get some coffee."

"I've had enough for today. I'm damp all through. There, give us a cigarette, Victor, old man. When are you going home?"

"Not for another hour. It's fine this afternoon, and I'm getting into decent shape. Look out, get off the track; here comes Fraulein Winkel. Damned elegant the way she manages her sled!"

"I'm cold all through. That's the worst of this place—the mists—it's a damp cold. Here, Foreman, look after this sled—and stick it somewhere so that I can get it without looking through a hundred and fifty others tomorrow morning."

They sat down at a small round table near the stove and ordered coffee. Victor sprawled in his chair, patting his little brown dog Bobo and looking, half laughingly, at Max.

"What's the matter, my dear? Isn't the world being nice and pretty?"

"I want my coffee, and I want to put my feet into my pocket—they're like stones. . . . Nothing to eat, thanks—the cake is like underdone india rubber here."

Fuchs and Wistuba came and sat at their table. Max half turned his back and stretched his feet out to the oven. The three other men all began talking at once—of the weather—of the record slide—of the fine condition of the Wald See for skating. Suddenly Fuchs looked at Max, raised his eyebrows and nodded across to Victor, who shook his head.

"Max doesn't feel well," he said, feeding the brown dog with broken lumps of sugar, "and nobody's to disturb him—I'm nurse."

"That's the first time I've ever known him off color," said Wistuba. "I've always imagined he had the better part of this world that could not be taken away from him. I think he says his prayers to the dear Lord for having spared him being taken home in seven basketsful tonight. It's a fool's game to risk your all that way and leave the nation desolate."

"Dry up," said Max. "You ought to be wheeled about on the snow in a baby carriage."

"Oh, no offense, I hope. Don't get nasty. . . . How's your wife, Victor?"

"She's not at all well. She hurt her head coming down the slide with Max on Sunday."

Recalling Facts

1. Max asked Victor for
   - □ a. some coffee.
   - □ b. a cigarette.
   - □ c. a sled.

2. Max asked to have
   - □ a. his sled waxed.
   - □ b. his sled stored.
   - □ c. Fuchs buy more cigarettes.

3. Bobo was the name of
   - □ a. a dog.
   - □ b. a sled.
   - □ c. anyone who fell off a sled.

4. The Wald See was a place for
   - □ a. eating.
   - □ b. smoking.
   - □ c. skating.

5. Victor's wife hurt her head sliding with
   - □ a. Fuchs.
   - □ b. Wistuba.
   - □ c. Max.

Understanding the Passage

6. Victor considered Max's sliding to be
   - □ a. rather dangerous.
   - □ b. a lot of harmless fun.
   - □ c. too expensive.

7. It appears that Max
   - □ a. enjoyed the damp, cold weather.
   - □ b. sometimes had trouble finding his sled.
   - □ c. wanted to slide longer.

8. After Max stopped sliding, he felt
   - □ a. tired but happy.
   - □ b. like getting more exercise.
   - □ c. cold and miserable.

9. The other three men
   - □ a. praised Max.
   - □ b. did not know Max.
   - □ c. teased Max.

10. The other three men did not share Max's love for
    - □ a. taking risks.
    - □ b. coffee and cigarettes.
    - □ c. the Wald See.

"Have you ever drawn a picture of a corpse?" asked Jamison next morning as I walked into his private room with a sketch of the proposed full page of the Zoo.

"No, and I don't want to," I replied, sullenly.

"Let me see your Central Park page," said Jamison in his gentle voice. I displayed it for him. It was worthless as a work of art but it pleased Jamison. I knew that it would.

"Can you finish it by this afternoon?" he asked.

"Oh, I suppose so," I said, wearily. "Anything else, Mr. Jamison?"

"The corpse," he replied. "I want a sketch by tomorrow—finished."

"What corpse?" I demanded, controlling myself as I met Jamison's soft eyes.

There was a mute duel of glances. Jamison passed his hand across his forehead with a slight lifting of the eyebrows.

"I shall want it as soon as possible," he said.

"Where is this corpse?" I asked.

"In the morgue—have you read the morning papers? No? Ah—as you very rightly observe you are too busy to read the morning papers. Young men must learn industry first, of course. What you are to do is this: the San Francisco police have sent out an alarm regarding the disappearance of a Miss Tufft—the millionaire's daughter, you know. Today a body was brought to the morgue here in New York. It has been identified as the missing young lady—by a diamond ring. Now I am sure that it isn't, and I'll show you why."

He picked up a pen and made a sketch of a ring on a margin of that morning's *Tribune.*

"That is the description of her ring as sent on from San Francisco. You notice the diamond is set in the center of the ring where the two gold serpents' *tails* cross!"

"Now the ring on the finger of the woman in the morgue is like this," and he rapidly sketched another ring where the diamond rested in the *fangs* of the two gold serpents.

"That is the difference," he said in his pleasant, even voice.

"Rings like that are common," said I. I then remembered that I had seen such a ring on the finger of the white-faced girl in the Park the evening before. Then a sudden thought took shape—perhaps that was the girl whose body lay in the morgue!

Recalling Facts

1. The narrator had just completed his sketch of the
   - ☐ a. Zoo.
   - ☐ b. morgue.
   - ☐ c. ring.

2. Jamison wanted the narrator to draw a picture of
   - ☐ a. an ill person.
   - ☐ b. an accident.
   - ☐ c. a corpse.

3. Miss Tufft was the daughter of a
   - ☐ a. gem dealer.
   - ☐ b. millionaire.
   - ☐ c. politician.

4. The missing young lady was identified by her
   - ☐ a. clothing.
   - ☐ b. dental records.
   - ☐ c. diamond ring.

5. Jamison's remarks made the narrator remember the girl he had seen
   - ☐ a. many years ago.
   - ☐ b. early last year.
   - ☐ c. the evening before.

Understanding the Passage

6. Jamison appeared to be the narrator's
   - ☐ a. best friend.
   - ☐ b. employer.
   - ☐ c. attorney.

7. Jamison wanted the narrator to
   - ☐ a. work as fast as possible.
   - ☐ b. identify the young girl.
   - ☐ c. get him the morning papers.

8. Miss Tufft's hometown was
   - ☐ a. New York.
   - ☐ b. San Francisco.
   - ☐ c. Chicago.

9. Jamison believed that the police
   - ☐ a. were on the right track.
   - ☐ b. were working much too slowly.
   - ☐ c. had incorrectly identified the corpse.

10. The narrator
   - ☐ a. thought he might have seen the dead woman before.
   - ☐ b. showed little interest in Jamison's idea.
   - ☐ c. knew how the young lady died.

"I admit I have had a drop. You must excuse me. I went into a beer shop on the way here, and as it was so hot I had a couple of bottles. It's hot, my boy."

Old Musatov took a shabby rag out of his pocket and wiped his shaven, battered face with it.

"I have come only for a minute, Borenka, my angel," he went on, not looking at his son, "about something very important. Excuse me, perhaps I am hindering you. Haven't you ten rubles, my dear, you could let me have till Tuesday? You see, I ought to have paid for my lodging yesterday, and money, you see! None! Not to save my life!"

Young Musatov went out without a word, and began whispering on the other side of the door with the landlady of the summer villa and his colleagues who had taken the villa with him. Three minutes later he came back, and without a word gave his father a ten-ruble note. The latter thrust it carelessly into his pocket without looking at it, and said:

"Thanks. Well, how are you getting on? It's a long time since we met."

"Yes, a long time, not since Easter."

"Half a dozen times I have been meaning to come to you, but I've never had time. First one thing, then another. It's simply awful! I'm talking nonsense though. All that's nonsense. Don't you believe me, Borenka. I said I would pay you back the ten rubles on Tuesday; don't believe that either. Don't believe a word I say. I have nothing to do at all; it's simply laziness, drunkenness, and I am ashamed to be seen in such clothes in the street. You must excuse me, Borenka. Here I have sent the girl to you three times for money and written you piteous letters. Thanks for the money, but don't believe the letters; I was telling fibs. I am ashamed to rob you, my angel. I know that you can scarcely make both ends meet yourself, but my impudence is too much for me. I am such a specimen of impudence—fit for a show! You must excuse me, Borenka. I tell you the truth, because I can't see your angel face without emotion."

A minute passed in silence. The old man heaved a deep sigh and said:

"You might treat me to a glass of beer perhaps."

Recalling Facts

1. Borenka was Musatov's
   - □ a. drinking partner.
   - □ b. son.
   - □ c. brother.

2. Musatov wanted to
   - □ a. borrow money.
   - □ b. have some food.
   - □ c. quit drinking.

3. Borenka and Musatov had not seen each other since
   - □ a. New Year's Day.
   - □ b. Easter.
   - □ c. Christmas.

4. Musatov called Borenka his
   - □ a. savior.
   - □ b. angel.
   - □ c. comrade.

5. Musatov asked Borenka to treat him to a glass of
   - □ a. vodka.
   - □ b. ale.
   - □ c. beer.

Understanding the Passage

6. Musatov was
   - □ a. out of money.
   - □ b. recovering from a beating.
   - □ c. getting married.

7. Apparently, Borenka
   - □ a. hated Musatov.
   - □ b. had given Musatov money before.
   - □ c. owed money for the villa.

8. Musatov had a hard time
   - □ a. hanging on to money.
   - □ b. telling the truth.
   - □ c. both a and b.

9. Apparently, Borenka was
   - □ a. rather poor himself.
   - □ b. unconcerned about Musatov's troubles.
   - □ c. dressed more poorly than Musatov.

10. Musatov seemed to be
    - □ a. in control of his life.
    - □ b. genuinely fond of Borenka.
    - □ c. overcoming his drinking problem.

A poor servant-girl was once traveling with the family with which she was in service through a great forest. When they were in the midst of it, robbers came out of the thicket, and murdered all they found. All perished together except the girl, who had jumped out of the carriage in a fright, and hidden herself behind a tree. When the robbers had gone away with their booty, she came out and beheld the great disaster. Then she began to weep bitterly. She cried, "What can a poor girl like me do now? I do not know how to get out of the forest. No human being lives in it, so I must certainly starve." She walked about and looked for a road, but could find none. When it was evening she seated herself under a tree, gave herself into God's keeping, and resolved to sit waiting there and not go away, no matter what happened. When, however, she had sat there for a while, a white dove came flying to her with a little golden key in its mouth. It put the little key in her hand, and said, "Do you see that great tree? Therein is a little lock; it opens with the tiny key, and there you will find food enough, and suffer no more hunger." The girl went to the tree and opened it. She found milk in a little dish and white bread to break into it, so that she could eat her fill. When she was satisfied, she said, "It is now the time when the hens at home go to roost. I am so tired I could go to bed too." Then the dove flew to her again. It brought another golden key in its bill, and said, "Open that tree there, and you will find a bed." So she opened it. She found a beautiful white bed and she prayed God to protect her during the night. She lay down and slept. In the morning the dove came for the third time. It again brought a little key and said, "Open that tree there, and you will find clothes." And when she opened it, she found garments beset with gold and with jewels, more splendid than those of any king's daughter. So she lived there for some time. The dove came every day and provided her with all she needed.

Recalling Facts

1. The robbers attacked the family
   - ☐ a. in the great forest.
   - ☐ b. along a town road.
   - ☐ c. near the coast.

2. The girl hid herself behind
   - ☐ a. the carriage.
   - ☐ b. a rock.
   - ☐ c. a tree.

3. The key carried by the white dove was
   - ☐ a. silver.
   - ☐ b. golden.
   - ☐ c. wooden.

4. Inside the first tree the girl found milk and
   - ☐ a. honey.
   - ☐ b. cookies.
   - ☐ c. bread.

5. The dove came to see the girl
   - ☐ a. twice.
   - ☐ b. three times.
   - ☐ c. every day.

Understanding the Passage

6. The robbers could best be described as
   - ☐ a. thoughtless.
   - ☐ b. bloodthirsty.
   - ☐ c. bumbling.

7. After viewing the disaster, the girl felt
   - ☐ a. relieved.
   - ☐ b. hopeless.
   - ☐ c. vengeful.

8. The dove knew that the girl
   - ☐ a. was in need.
   - ☐ b. had never been in a forest before.
   - ☐ c. was a friend of the robbers.

9. After a while the girl
   - ☐ a. adjusted to her life in the forest.
   - ☐ b. made her home with the dove.
   - ☐ c. lost the keys the dove had given her.

10. The dove could best be described as
    - ☐ a. annoying.
    - ☐ b. helpful.
    - ☐ c. sad.

They scrambled downwards, splashed across stream, up rocks and along the trail of the other side. Romero's black horse stopped, looked down quizzically at the fallen trees, then stepped over lightly. The Princess's sorrel followed, carefully. But Miss Cummins's buckskin made a fuss, and had to be got round.

In the same silence, save for the clinking of the horses and the splashing as the trail crossed stream, they worked their way upwards in the tight, tangled shadow of the canyon.

They were getting fairly high. Then again they dipped and crossed stream, the horses stepping gingerly across a tangle of fallen, frail aspen stems, then suddenly floundering in a mass of rocks. The black emerged ahead, his black tail waving. The Princess let her mare find her own footing; then she too emerged from the clatter. She rode on after the black. Then came a great frantic rattle of the buckskin behind. The Princess was aware of Romero's dark face looking round, with a strange, demonlike watchfulness, before she herself looked round, to see the buckskin scrambling rather lamely beyond the rocks, with one of his pale buff knees already red with blood.

"He almost went down!" called Miss Cummins.

But Romero was already out of the saddle and hastening down the path. He made quiet little noises to the buckskin, and began examining the cut knee.

"Is he hurt?" cried Miss Cummins anxiously, and she climbed hastily down.

"Oh, my goodness!" she cried, as she saw the blood running down the slender buff leg of the horse in a thin trickle. "Isn't that *awful?*" She spoke in a stricken voice, and her face was white.

Romero was still carefully feeling the knee of the buckskin. Then he made him walk a few paces. At last he stood up straight and shook his head. "Not very bad!" he said. "Nothing broken."

Again he bent and worked at the knee. Then he looked up at the Princess. "He can go on," he said. "It's not bad."

"What, go on up here?" cried Miss Cummins. "How many hours?"

"About five," said Romero simply.

"Five hours!" cried Miss Cummins. "A horse with a lame knee! And a steep mountain! Why-y!"

"Yes, it's pretty steep up there," said Romero, pushing back his hat and staring fixedly at the bleeding knee.

Recalling Facts

1. Romero was riding a
   - ☐ a. buckskin.
   - ☐ b. sorrel.
   - ☐ c. black horse.

2. The Princess and her companions were traveling
   - ☐ a. up through a canyon.
   - ☐ b. along a road.
   - ☐ c. through the desert.

3. The buckskin cut its
   - ☐ a. knee.
   - ☐ b. neck.
   - ☐ c. nose.

4. Romero said the horse's injury was
   - ☐ a. life threatening.
   - ☐ b. fairly extensive.
   - ☐ c. not serious.

5. Romero estimated that they would not reach their destination for
   - ☐ a. two hours.
   - ☐ b. five hours.
   - ☐ c. eight hours.

Understanding the Passage

6. The buckskin seemed quite
   - ☐ a. uncomfortable on the rugged trail.
   - ☐ b. content when off a marked path.
   - ☐ c. nervous around the Princess.

7. The Princess had
   - ☐ a. never ridden a horse before.
   - ☐ b. faith in her horse.
   - ☐ c. great love for Romero.

8. Romero felt that
   - ☐ a. Miss Cummins should turn around and go home.
   - ☐ b. he should put the horse out of its misery.
   - ☐ c. the buckskin would be all right.

9. Miss Cummins's reaction to the horse's injury was one of
   - ☐ a. disgust.
   - ☐ b. resignation.
   - ☐ c. horror.

10. Romero believed the journey
    - ☐ a. was well planned.
    - ☐ b. would never end.
    - ☐ c. should continue.

Answer Key

Progress Graph

Pacing Graph

Answer Key

1	1. b	2. c	3. a	4. b	5. b	6. a	7. b	8. b	9. c	10. b
2	1. c	2. a	3. c	4. b	5. c	6. b	7. b	8. a	9. b	10. a
3	1. b	2. c	3. b	4. a	5. c	6. a	7. a	8. a	9. b	10. a
4	1. b	2. c	3. a	4. c	5. a	6. a	7. b	8. b	9. b	10. b
5	1. c	2. b	3. b	4. a	5. b	6. a	7. a	8. c	9. a	10. c
6	1. b	2. b	3. b	4. a	5. b	6. a	7. c	8. a	9. a	10. b
7	1. c	2. a	3. c	4. c	5. b	6. b	7. b	8. b	9. a	10. c
8	1. c	2. c	3. b	4. a	5. a	6. b	7. a	8. c	9. c	10. b
9	1. b	2. a	3. c	4. a	5. b	6. c	7. a	8. a	9. b	10. c
10	1. b	2. c	3. c	4. a	5. c	6. a	7. b	8. a	9. c	10. c
11	1. c	2. c	3. b	4. b	5. b	6. a	7. a	8. c	9. b	10. a
12	1. a	2. b	3. c	4. c	5. c	6. a	7. c	8. c	9. a	10. c
13	1. c	2. a	3. b	4. b	5. c	6. b	7. a	8. a	9. c	10. b
14	1. c	2. b	3. c	4. b	5. a	6. a	7. b	8. b	9. b	10. b
15	1. a	2. b	3. c	4. b	5. b	6. b	7. b	8. c	9. a	10. b
16	1. b	2. c	3. a	4. a	5. c	6. a	7. c	8. c	9. c	10. a
17	1. b	2. a	3. c	4. b	5. c	6. a	7. b	8. c	9. c	10. b
18	1. b	2. b	3. c	4. b	5. c	6. c	7. b	8. a	9. b	10. a
19	1. c	2. b	3. a	4. b	5. a	6. c	7. b	8. b	9. c	10. a
20	1. b	2. c	3. b	4. a	5. c	6. a	7. b	8. b	9. a	10. c
21	1. c	2. b	3. a	4. b	5. c	6. b	7. b	8. a	9. c	10. a
22	1. c	2. c	3. a	4. b	5. b	6. a	7. b	8. b	9. c	10. a
23	1. c	2. a	3. a	4. c	5. b	6. c	7. a	8. b	9. c	10. a
24	1. c	2. a	3. b	4. b	5. b	6. b	7. a	8. a	9. b	10. b
25	1. b	2. c	3. a	4. b	5. c	6. b	7. c	8. c	9. a	10. b

26	1. c	2. b	3. c	4. a	5. b	6. b	7. b	8. c	9. b	10. b
27	1. b	2. c	3. c	4. c	5. a	6. a	7. c	8. b	9. b	10. b
28	1. b	2. c	3. c	4. a	5. c	6. b	7. c	8. c	9. c	10. c
29	1. c	2. b	3. a	4. a	5. c	6. a	7. b	8. c	9. b	10. a
30	1. b	2. a	3. c	4. c	5. a	6. a	7. c	8. b	9. a	10. b
31	1. a	2. b	3. b	4. c	5. b	6. a	7. b	8. c	9. c	10. a
32	1. b	2. a	3. a	4. b	5. b	6. a	7. c	8. c	9. a	10. b
33	1. b	2. c	3. a	4. b	5. b	6. a	7. c	8. b	9. b	10. b
34	1. c	2. a	3. c	4. b	5. b	6. c	7. a	8. a	9. b	10. a
35	1. c	2. a	3. a	4. b	5. b	6. c	7. a	8. b	9. c	10. a
36	1. c	2. b	3. a	4. b	5. a	6. a	7. a	8. a	9. b	10. c
37	1. c	2. a	3. b	4. c	5. c	6. a	7. c	8. c	9. b	10. a
38	1. b	2. a	3. c	4. c	5. c	6. b	7. c	8. a	9. b	10. b
39	1. c	2. a	3. c	4. c	5. b	6. c	7. b	8. a	9. c	10. c
40	1. c	2. a	3. a	4. c	5. b	6. c	7. b	8. a	9. b	10. b
41	1. c	2. b	3. b	4. c	5. a	6. a	7. b	8. c	9. b	10. b
42	1. a	2. c	3. b	4. c	5. c	6. a	7. a	8. a	9. b	10. b
43	1. a	2. b	3. c	4. c	5. c	6. c	7. b	8. c	9. c	10. a
44	1. b	2. b	3. b	4. a	5. b	6. c	7. b	8. c	9. b	10. b
45	1. b	2. a	3. c	4. a	5. b	6. a	7. c	8. c	9. b	10. b
46	1. b	2. b	3. a	4. c	5. c	6. a	7. b	8. c	9. c	10. a
47	1. a	2. c	3. b	4. c	5. c	6. b	7. a	8. b	9. c	10. a
48	1. b	2. a	3. b	4. b	5. c	6. a	7. b	8. c	9. a	10. b
49	1. a	2. c	3. b	4. c	5. c	6. b	7. b	8. a	9. a	10. b
50	1. c	2. a	3. a	4. c	5. b	6. a	7. b	8. c	9. c	10. c

Progress Graph (1–25)

Directions: Write your comprehension score in the box under the selection number. Then put an x on the line above each box to show your reading time and words-per-minute reading rate.

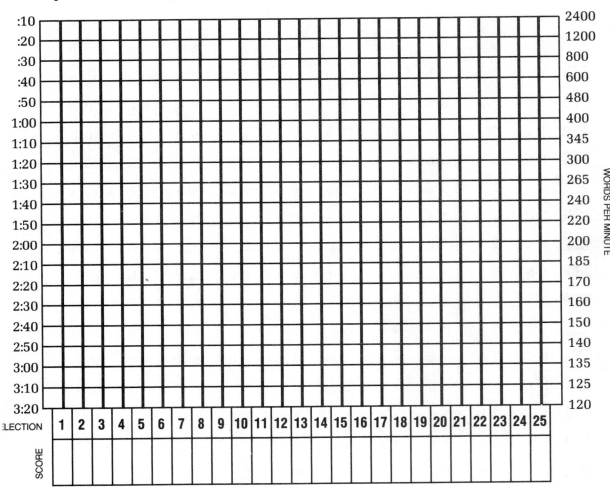

WORDS PER MINUTE

SELECTION	1	2	3	4	5	6	7	8	9	10	11	12	13	14	15	16	17	18	19	20	21	22	23	24	25
SCORE																									

Progress Graph (26–50)

Directions: Write your comprehension score in the box under the selection number. Then put an x on the line above each box to show your reading time and words-per-minute reading rate.

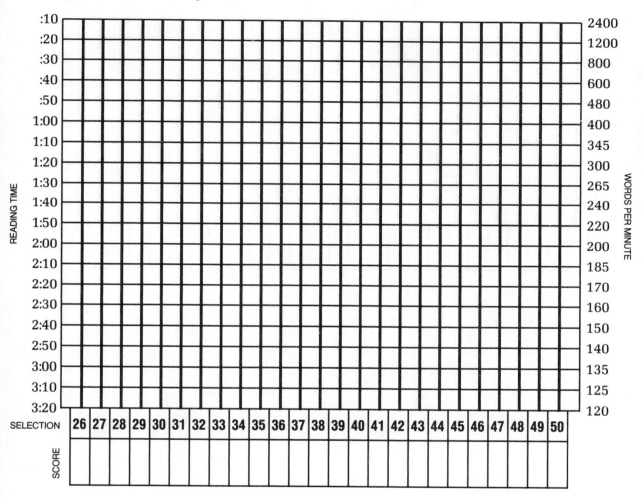

READING TIME

WORDS PER MINUTE

Time	WPM
:10	2400
:20	1200
:30	800
:40	600
:50	480
1:00	400
1:10	345
1:20	300
1:30	265
1:40	240
1:50	220
2:00	200
2:10	185
2:20	170
2:30	160
2:40	150
2:50	140
3:00	135
3:10	125
3:20	120

SELECTION: 26 27 28 29 30 31 32 33 34 35 36 37 38 39 40 41 42 43 44 45 46 47 48 49 50

SCORE

Pacing Graph

Directions: In the boxes labeled "Pace" along the bottom of the graph, write your words-per-minute rate. On the vertical line above each box, put an x to indicate your comprehension score.

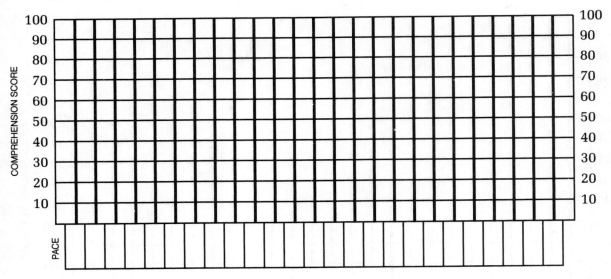